the Celts

of the British Isles

Also by David Ross
Scotland: History of a Nation
Ancient Scotland

THE CELTS

of the British Isles

*From the Earliest Times
to the Viking Invasion*

David Ross

GEDDES & GROSSET

Published 2004 by Geddes & Grosset,
David Dale House, New Lanark, ML11 9DJ, Scotland

ISBN 1 84205 356 6

Printed in Poland, OZGraf S.A.

Contents

Introduction

'Your romanticism is one vast self-delusion, and it blinds your eye to the real thing. We have got to clear it out, and with it all the damnable humbug of the Kelt.'

Mr McCunn, who spelt the word with a soft 'C', was puzzled. 'I thought a kelt was a kind of a no-weel fish,' he interposed.

John Buchan, *Huntingtower*

' "Celtic", of any sort is . . . a magic bag, into which anything may be put, and out of which almost anything may come.'

J. R. R. Tolkien, 'English and Welsh', from *Angles and Britons*

We owe the modern use of the words 'Celt' and 'Celtic' to one of the greatest Scotsmen, George Buchanan (1506–82), the Renaissance scholar, poet, and historian. His work led to the adoption of the term 'Celtic' to define the group of languages that included his native Gaelic, as well as Welsh, Cornish, Breton, and the Gaelic of Ireland. In this way, 'Celt', which in ancient history applied only to peoples on the continent of Europe, was brought into the British tradition. The usage was confirmed with the publication of *Archaeologica Britannica* by the Welsh scholar, Edward Lhuyd, in 1707. Lhuyd wrote of 'the Celtique' as the living language of Wales, Cornwall and Brittany. He had been inspired by a French work published in

1703 by the Breton Paul-Yves Pezron, *Antiquité de la nation et de langue des Celtes, autrement appelez Gaulois,* Antiquity of the Nation and Language of the Celts, otherwise called Gauls.

It was these 18th-century books that introduced some sections of the population of the British Isles to the idea that they were Celts. The notion took root with great speed and developed its own momentum. Lhuyd had used the term to apply only to languages, and to people only as speakers of those languages. Before long, however, it was being used in a different way. A linguistic tradition reaching back into the past before the Roman invasion of Britain – and far before the arrival of the Anglo-Saxons – had been established. It was easy to extend this to suppose a cultural and, indeed, a racial tradition as well, with an equally long pedigree. The appeal of such a thought to the Scots, Irish, and Welsh is obvious. For hundreds of years they had been defining their own identities in contrast and opposition to England. Here was a splendid opportunity to underline that difference and to give it a sense of authenticity. As a further bonus, the 'Celtic' tradition showed the Anglo-Saxons as Johnny-come-latelies in the British Isles, and as a mere late-developed branch of the Teutons. But, among the English, too, the revelation of a 'Celtic' prehistory had both a romantic and a scholarly appeal for many. There was a difficulty, however, though everyone chose to ignore it. In classical times, those Greek and Latin writers who mentioned the British Isles had never suggested that the inhabitants of the islands were Celts. They used this term exclusively for peoples of the European continent. Moreover, Julius Caesar had reported that the inhabitants of the larger island believed they had always lived there.

How then did the Celtic languages – and, by extension, Celtic culture and Celtic people – reach the British Isles? For over 200 years, there was only one answer – by migration, or invasion. This was not an unreasonable idea; after all, the invasions of the Normans, Anglo-Saxons, and Romans were all known historical events. To propose earlier invasions as a means of cultural and racial change seemed perfectly natural. So strong was the background idea that any archaeological evidence – pottery, buildings, weapons, tools – was interpreted unquestioningly in the context of invasion.

Though many scholars expressed some reservations about this, it was only in the 1960s that the assumption was authoritatively challenged. A paper entitled 'The invasion hypothesis in British prehistory' from one of Britain's leading archaeologists, professor Grahame Clark, pointed out the lack of actual evidence for large invasive movements. Since then, prehistorians have discarded the invasion theory of Celticisation in favour of a different process. This is 'cultural dissemination' – in which new ideas, ways of thinking, or food-producing, or worshipping, or building, or speaking, spread very gradually across the inhabited landscape. They are passed on, not by conquest and forceful imposition, but by learning and imitation. Recent historical models can be found for this process too, including the gradual decline of Gaelic speech, in favour of English, across Scotland and Ireland from the 13th to the 19th century. On a remoter and far larger scale, professor Colin Renfrew traced the gradual spread of agriculture and, with it, the Indo-European languages, across the face of Europe during the millennia from around 6500 to 3500BCE (see Chapter One). His book, *Archaeology and Language*, published in 1987, is a key text for what he calls the 'processual approach' to cultural change. It is very relevant to Celtic studies.

The questions of how 'insular Celtic culture' arose and of whether there is an ethnic 'Celtic' component in the peoples of the British archipelago – 'British' is used in this book in the sense of the ancient name, and not the 18th-century Scottish-English political amalgam – raise emotive political and nationalistic overtones. The concept of migration-invasion dates from much earlier than the 18th century. Six hundred years earlier, a range of ancient legendary sources were combined in the *Lebor Gabála Érenn*, 'Book of the Taking of Ireland', which describes six successive invasions, or arrivals, of peoples or tribes in Ireland. It was long supposed that, however altered and added to by propaganda and prejudice, these stories of an origin in the East must contain a substratum of fact. Meanwhile, royal genealogies were rigged to show descent from legendary figures. Resonant names, though hazy personalities, like Scota, Míl Espáine, Fergus mór MacErc, Emrys Wledig, Arthur, Nechtan macMorbet, underlie the self-perception of Irish, Scots, and Welsh as 'Celtic' peoples.

There are great gaps, many unproved assertions, many conflicting pieces of evidence, in the charting of human events in Britain and Ireland before the Common Era (CE), and in the ensuing millennium to 1000CE. But, in the past 20 or so years, modern archaeology, armed with a far greater battery of technical resources than before, has been establishing a clearer picture of ancient life in these islands. In the pattern that emerges, continuity is far more significant than sudden change, and assimilation of ideas is more apparent than imposition from outside. Some long-held or cherished notions no longer fit this emerging pattern, whether about Celtic aspects or others, and must be discarded. But what is really exciting is the way in which such research now reveals a process of continuity that links us not only to the practitioners of Celtic art and culture but to further ancestors beyond them, the megalith builders, and maybe farther still, to the hunter-fisher-gatherers whose small groups wandered across the landscape when there was no British archipelago but a single landmass, a great peninsula reaching out from northwestern Europe.

CHAPTER ONE

First and Later Beginnings

No one knows when the British Isles were first inhabited by humans. Settlement began before they were islands at all, when a land bridge linked England to France and western Scotland to northern Ireland, and the North Sea was a huge waterlogged marsh. The earliest human occupancy has been put at 450,000 years ago, far back in the early Stone Age of human history. The Ice Age – the most recent period of geological history – had already begun. Three times successive ice sheets annihilated life and its record in Scotland, Ireland, and Northern England. But England south of the Thames escaped glaciation, even in the farthest extent of the ice, and the final advance of the ice sheet did not pass a line that can be traced from Fishguard, round the Welsh uplands, up to Chester, across to north Yorkshire, and then south again, a few miles inland from the coastline, to north Norfolk. Ireland was almost entirely covered by ice at this time, apart from the southeast and a few northern and western peninsulas. The exposed landscapes would have resembled subarctic tundra, and the climate would have been inhospitable to creatures and plants unadapted to the cold. It is likely that there was a break in human habitation at this time, although the example of the Inuit in recent centuries shows that human communities can subsist in subarctic conditions. Through the centuries of the ice's gradual withdrawal, humans again began to take possession of the ground. By the early stages of the Holocene period, about 10,000 years ago, the entire region was free of permanent ice cover. Scotland and Ireland were separated by a narrow sea but the English Channel had not yet formed.

Even if earlier human communities had survived the Ice Age, they would not have survived the arrival of new explorers. Our own subspecies, *Homo sapiens sapiens*, appeared in Europe about 35,000 years ago. Its penetration northwards and north-westwards would have been governed by the position of the ice frontier. This era is termed by geologists the Weichselian, and corresponds to the last period of British glaciation. At this time, hunters could have moved far into England, but Wales, Ireland, and Scotland would have been largely or wholly icebound. The ice-free terrain was a rich hunting ground. Among larger mammals, bison, mammoth, and reindeer were to be found on land, and the sea teemed with a diversity and number of creatures that is hardly imaginable compared with the human-created marine desert of today. Earlier human subspecies, like *Homo sapiens neanderthalis*, were destroyed by the advent of *Homo sapiens sapiens*, whose brainpower and capacity for creating and using tools were matched by a spirit of competition, anxiety, and aggression with which we are still highly familiar.

What has such very early history to do with the Celts, who are identified with a far later period of human development? The answer is – a very great deal. In exploring the history of the peoples of the British Isles, it is essential to bear these Stone-Age inhabitants in mind. They are part of our ancestry. We have no reason to suppose that the first permanent settlers after the Ice Age were ever annihilated or displaced by natural or human-driven events. Continuity, not conquest or invasion, is the key-word. Through the long slow millennia of social and technical evolution, the population gradually grew larger and spread in small groups across the countryside. These many generations, layered each upon its predecessor like geological strata, remain silent and anonymous. Silent because we do not know what language or languages were spoken; anonymous because we have no record of names, either of peoples or individuals, and very little other evidence. But these were human societies, vibrant, questioning, experimenting, capable of memory and strategy. Only the archaeological record speaks for them, and though we have become increasingly adept at interpreting it, we still know little of their lives, their societies, and their thoughts and beliefs. What we have is, rather, a few islands of information surrounded by a sea of inference and speculation.

The broad lines of development are clear, however. Around 15,000 years ago, the period of human development in north-west Europe was the Upper Palaeolithic, the second phase of the Stone Age, not as immensely long as the Lower Palaeolithic, which preceded it, though still measured in thousands of years. But the numbers of humans were very few. The British Isles, even after the ice had largely receded, were not a favoured habitat for humanity. Only the scantiest remnants of early human occupancy have been found from this time, and it seems that the people favoured caves as dwelling sites, rather than making temporary camps, like the earlier inhabitants. Christopher and Jacquetta Hawkes, in *Prehistoric Britain*, comparing the Palaeolithic inhabitants of Britain to those of south-west France, wrote:

> 'that part of Western Europe destined to become the British Isles was too remote, too ice-ridden, to support so high a standard of life. Probably the population never amounted to more than a few hundred souls, mainly absorbed in the quest for food. Caves in Derbyshire, north and south Wales, the Wye Valley and the Mendips, were occupied, but the majority only sporadically and for short periods; artistic content is extremely rare, and even flint and bone tools are generally poor and scanty.'

Britain offers no cave paintings from this time, only one or two animal and human images scratched into bone. Ireland, where the deep-water channel that has since widened into the Irish Sea had already opened up with the withdrawal of the ice, was probably as yet uninhabited by either *Homo neanderthalis* or *Homo sapiens sapiens* – an Eden still awaiting its human masters.

The way of life was that of hunter-gatherers. It was an opportunist existence, in that it depended on catching animals, fish, and birds, and on finding edible plants and berries, but based already on long-and-hard-won knowledge and experience. They made and used their own tools from stone and, no doubt, wood and bone. The number of habitable caves in Britain is not great and, even though the people lived in makeshift shelters around the cave mouth, using the inner area for shelter and storage, they gradually spread away from the shelter of caves to open camp sites. Around them, in a way that might have been scarcely perceptible from generation to generation, the landscape, climate, and vegetation were changing. For more than 2000 years after the ice sheet had retreated, the earth remained frozen, apart from a shallow surface layer that thawed in summer and produced a vegetation of dwarf shrubs, mosses, and lichens that in turn supported insect and bird life, and wide-ranging migrant herds of deer. Many square miles of such a landscape would be needed to support even a tiny human community.

By around 8500BCE, the permafrost had gone, and a more temperate climate was encouraging a much more varied and vigorous vegetation. From then, changes can be traced that lead into the Mesolithic period, or Middle Stone Age. The growth of forest cover, with hazel and oak trees, had encouraged the arrival and distribution of woodland animals: elk, beaver, roe deer, pig, wild ox, and wolf. The torrents and floods of the postglacial era had settled to a more stable pattern of rivers and lakes, though it was a much marshier landscape than would be the case later, with far more pools and meres. In the more settled and temperate waters, fish remained abundant and shellfish thrived. Now a more limited range of territory could support a human community. The Mesolithic inhabitants did not have a settled place of residence but moved their camps around, within an established area perhaps as large as 500 square kilometres (194 square miles), in order to best exploit the resources, reoccupying the same sites on a seasonal basis. It is likely that, towards the end of the Mesolithic period at least, they were also burning sections of forest, to create clearings where new secondary growth of berry-bearing bushes would spring up, and also perhaps to drive animals into areas where they could be trapped. Their tools were becoming increasingly specialised.

The sea level was steadily rising, by up to 50m (150ft), but around much of the coastline, especially in the north and west, where the trillions of tons of ice pressure had pushed down the land surface, the process of isostatic uplift was raising the shoreline faster than the sea could encroach, producing the raised beaches of Scotland and Ireland at the same time as, in the south and east, the North Sea and the English Channel were forming, and the estuaries of Devon and Cornwall were filling with tidal waters. A group of islands was emerging, off the coast of the continent: two very large ones and many smaller ones. From around 6000BCE, access to or from the continent could only be gained by crossing the sea. But, by this time, the art of the dugout boat was already known to the inhabitants and, in the millennium before, vast forests had grown up across the land, offering an unlimited supply of trees long and thick enough for the purpose.

The separation of the islands from the continent was of momentous significance. Once it was no longer possible to make the overland crossing, the process of insular development began, affecting all forms of life, human, animal, and vegetable. Until that point, human culture in Britain was closely related to that in northern Europe, and the name Maglemosian, from Magle Mose ('great marsh') in Denmark has been given to these forest dwellers. Typical of their technology was the microlith, or small stone blade. These blades were fixed into wooden handles to serve a variety of purposes from cutting edges to spearheads. They also used larger flint pieces to make axe heads capable of cutting down trees, and adzes to hollow out their canoes from tree trunks. Bone and horn tools have also been found from this time: elk horns seem to have been used as pickaxes, and sharpened bones as harpoon heads. By the time the Mesolithic era was merging into the Neolithic, stone blades being made in Britain had a distinctive shape, unlike contemporary continental products.

The population was still very small, and few Mesolithic sites have been found. But, if a group of, say, 30 people required some 500 square kilometres (200 square miles) of land, then an area the size of Kent could have supported a little over 200 persons and the entire population of Great Britain, allowing for inhospitable upland, could have been little more than 10,000. Among the best-known sites is Star Carr, in Yorkshire, a site periodically occupied by around 25 people; a platform of felled birch logs and branches by the side of a lake now filled with peat deposits. This and other sites have enabled archaeologists to establish, or infer, a number of details about the lives of the inhabitants. They wore animal skins and furs, secured by bone pins, and had decorative beads of amber, stone, and deer teeth. They used bows as well as spears for hunting. Deer skulls with horns attached were found at Star Carr, and speculation as to their use has included hunting (where the horns worn by the hunters might have been seen as attracting the real deer) or in some kind of ritual procedure.

It seems to have been in the Mesolithic period that regular human habitation spread to Scotland and Ireland. How this happened is not quite clear, though the obvious route is overland from England via the Lowlands around Carlisle and through the passes of the Southern Uplands. Mesolithic settlements have been found in east Fife, and on the west at Oban and on the Hebridean isle of Oronsay, but not in between. Access by sea is not impossible; Mesolithic families travelled light. These western inhabitants have been described in one book as 'specialist fishermen', but whether they brought their speciality with them or acquired it *in situ* is impossible to say. In any case, their midden heaps reveal that they existed on chiefly on a marine diet of shellfish, sea fish, and seals. The discarded shells of limpets, whelks, and oysters are left in vast amounts on Oronsay. Smaller similar deposits have been found at Mesolithic coastal sites on the southern coasts of England and Wales.

From west and southwest Scotland, the Irish coast can clearly be seen, and it is generally assumed that the first settlers in Ireland crossed the narrow sea here. If so, it was the first of numerous transfers of population, in both directions, between these two landmasses, and this was the time that the western sea became the focus of Hebridean-Irish links and connections, which would continue until the 16th century CE (although Scotland, Ireland, and the Hebrides would not be political or social entities for thousands of years to come).

Certainly, the first reliable evidence of human occupancy in Ireland comes from the Mesolithic period, around 6000BCE. At Mount Sandel, above the River Bann, there was a community of hunter-gatherers, who lived in big circular huts, about 6m (20ft) in diameter. Sapling stems supported roofs of reed or foliage, and there was a central hearth. Like the settlements across the sea, it was not a permanent village but a transient, seasonal one. The relative density of such early sites in the northeast suggests that the first inhabitants came over the short sea route from western or southwestern Scotland, but Mesolithic sites are found as far south as Cork.

Eight thousand years ago, then, the larger British islands, and some of the lesser ones, were inhabited by humans. The density was scanty in the extreme; estimates of the total population by the end of the Mesolithic era are around 25,000. Nothing is known about the Mesolithic culture or cultures. Small isolated population groups might imply a degree of inbreeding in the population; but perhaps ways and means had been evolved to avoid this. Formal or informal intergroup meetings and encounters must have happened. A group that had no source of flints on its territory would have to find them somewhere else; though the mass production of flints is a feature of Neolithic times, the beginnings of the process probably lie in the Mesolithic. There are no preserved signs of cult and ritual, apart from the Star Carr deer masks. Oddly, there is more evidence from the preceding late Palaeolithic age. In the Paviland Cave in the Gower Peninsula, South Wales, a ceremonially buried body dating back to this period was found. At first it was wrongly identified as a 'red lady' but, in fact, it was a young man, whose bones had been smeared with red ochre. He was wearing a necklace of wolf and reindeer teeth (predator and herbivore combined); other ornaments were present, as well as a mammoth's skull. Red ochring of human remains was also found in Maglemosian burial sites in Denmark, from a much later date.

Mesolithic existence, close to, almost still a part of, nature, was a way of life that required an element of stasis – enough babies to maintain the community but not too many to share finite resources, and so impede mobility. Examination of human remains from the time does not suggest that they were a very healthy population: life expectancy rarely went beyond the 30s, and tooth decay, arthritis, and rheumatism were common. Centuries passed, uncounted by the inhabitants, as far as we know, but then the pace of change began to speed up. East of the Mediterranean, communities had begun to learn, and to pass on, some knowledge of agriculture. Slowly, at a rate of only about eight kilometres (five miles) in each human generation, elements of this knowledge were transmitted northwards and westwards. It was not an even process. People living on trading routes acquired it while their neighbours in the hills beyond continued to use the spear rather than the spade (or rather, the soil-scratching stick known as an ard, the ancestor of the plough).

Before 6000BCE, farming was established in Greece. Wheat, peas, and vetches were their crops, and they kept sheep and goats; perhaps also cattle and pigs. For a community to take up farming, after such a long history of hunting and fishing, was a major change. The process can be clearly dated: by 3500BCE, farming techniques had reached as far as the Orkney Islands, but the way in which it happened can only be reconstructed by hypothesis. Farming brought change to the immemorial nomadic way of life. Its practice spread into Ireland and Britain at much the same time, in a process complete by around 2500BCE. By this time, the western Europeans were benefiting from the long experience of the inhabitants of the Near East, where forms of agriculture had been developing since around 10000BCE. In *Neolithic Britain and Ireland*, Caroline Malone writes that, whatever the means, 'fully domestic plants and animals, and the technology and know-how to deal with them, did arrive in Britain as a complete subsistence package.' This practical knowledge, as well as actual animals, was imported from the coasts of France and Spain, and the longer sea route from northern Spain and northwest France was probably a more important conduit than the Straits of Dover. Apart from the importation of already-domesticated stock, indigenous wild pigs and horses were probably also domesticated. In the British Isles, where the temperate climate encouraged the growth of lush grass, cattle seem to have thrived especially, and, along with pigs, were the main stock animal, while sheep and goats were predominant in continental Europe. Dogs were kept, of a terrier-like type that may have been used for catching small animals and ground birds. Rabbits were, as yet, unknown to the islands, but rats and mice were probably already attracted to the food supplies available in human settlements. The community now had to stay in one place for long enough to plant and raise crops, to harvest them and to store the yield, both for food and for next year's seed. It followed that more permanent and substantial buildings were needed. In many places, ground had to be cleared of trees and stones to make small fields. For the first time, the people were making an investment in their territory, and this must have resulted in a change of attitude to the land. Farming was also hard work, of a kind that required a long-term coordinated approach very different from the briefer organisation of a hunt. It was an act of faith, in that the placing of seeds or seedlings in the soil was trusted to bring forth full-grown plants; new forms of social ritual were called for to make sense of this mystery. The reward was an easily accessible supply of basic food, of a higher quality than the people had known before and in a greater quantity. In particular, it could provide reserves that helped feed the community through the winter, which must always have been a period of hunger and the risk of starvation. Farming and hunting-gathering were not mutually exclusive: there was plenty of land and time for both.

In the famous model elaborated by professor Colin Renfrew in 1987, knowledge of farming techniques spread across Europe in a slow uneven wave in the course of the centuries between 6000 and 3500BCE. He saw this knowledge as a combination of two processes. One was the passing-on of information, the copying of techniques, and the trading of seeds and animals. In this way, a nonfarming community could learn farming practice from its neighbours. The other way was through the expansion of population. Since farming, and the settled community, could support more births, the population would increase. Eventually, it would increase to a point where the farming techniques could no longer support everyone. Every year, therefore, a few people, already well versed in farming methods, would move into empty land, clear and plant, and form the nucleus of a new community. Renfrew wrote:

' . . . the new economy of farming allowed the population in each area to rise, over just a few centuries from perhaps 0.1 persons per square kilometre to something like 5 or 10 per square kilometre [in modern terms, still a very light density]. As the model predicts, with only small, local movements of twenty or thirty kilometres, this would gradually result in the peopling of the whole of Europe by a farming population, the descendants of the first European farmers.'

Lord Renfrew places most reliance on the new generation, rather than on learning. This is quite reasonable, because the Mesolithic population was so small and thinly spread. The farmers needed less territory. Communities still practising a Mesolithic lifestyle could find themselves gradually encroached upon by agriculturists who were more numerous and who had vested interests to defend – the result might be a fight, or absorption, or a mixture of both. But Renfrew's wave model is also intended to explain the emergence of the languages spoken in Europe today. This is a vital question in exploring the history of the peoples who have been labelled as Celtic.

In the late 18th century, Sir William Jones, a brilliant linguist who had already written a grammar of Persian, was working as a judge in British-ruled Bengal. He was first to point out the correspondences between Sanskrit, the ancient language of India, and Greek and Latin, the 'classical' languages of Europe. These, he wrote, were 'so strong, indeed, that no philologist could examine them all three, without believing them to have sprung from some common source, which, perhaps, no longer exists.' Jones's observation lies at the basis of language history. Since then, scholars have established that most of the languages of Europe can be grouped together in a small number of linguistic families that share certain key features. The process of language development has continued within historical times and can be traced through preserved writing and place names. The gradual divergence of Scottish and Irish Gaelic from the eleventh century is a case in point; the development of modern English from Middle English and Old English, over a period of 1000 years, is another. It is only necessary to look at a few pages of Chaucer's *Canterbury Tales*, from the 14th century, and of the narrative poem 'Beowulf', from the 8th century, to see that the language is the same, yet with many differences. The origins of English lie in the languages spoken by the Anglian and Saxon tribes, who settled in England from the sixth century. These, in turn, were very similar to the speech of other Germanic tribes, which, in continental Europe, have evolved into German and Dutch. Some other Germanic languages, like Gothic, were dying out at that same time. It has been established that the Germanic languages stem from a common ancestral language, which has been given the name Indo-Germanic. This, in turn, can be traced back towards a parent language, or group of closely related languages, known as Proto-Indo-European. This ancient speech is thought to have been used by nomadic peoples in southern Russia, around 4000BCE. Its use spread southwards and westwards, modified by the passage of time, local environment, and interaction with pre-existent languages not of Indo-European origin. Sanskrit was the first Indo-European language to be written, and so preserves many older features.

The Celtic languages also form a family within the wider Indo-European group. We will return to the question of language, so crucial to the identity of Celtic peoples. But in the Mesolithic era, Celtic and Germanic alike were still far in the future. The inhabitants of the British Isles were then speaking languages of which no trace remains.

The wave model of culture dissemination is a very plausible explanation for the spread of cultural practices. Renfrew himself insisted on the fact that, in its basic expression, it is a highly simplified model of a very complicated and lengthy process, which is affected by wars, politics, plagues, famines, and many other aspects of social life. It is such an appealing solution that it can be hard to remember how recent it is. Before the 1970s, archaeologists and ancient historians were much more inclined to believe that cultural changes were imposed by one group upon others. In one form, the invasion theory could be a relatively peaceful process, of a new population spreading into a thinly populated countryside and either absorbing the existing inhabitants or displacing them into other territories, in a speeded-up version of the wave model. In another form, it could be a violent imposition of one culture upon another, enforced by superior weapons or tighter social organisation, or both.

CHAPTER TWO

Neolithic Farmers, Fishermen, and Foresters

If we follow the wave model of agricultural development in its progress across Europe, its methods being adapted to various climates and altitudes, we eventually come to a time, around 3500BCE, when knowledge of farming was in the possession of the people who lived on the western edges of the North Sea. Here, where the theoretical wave meets the real saltwater waves, is perhaps the severest test of the theory. Beyond the sea, only 32 kilometres (20 miles) away at the narrowest point, lies the Atlantic archipelago, islands thickly forested with deciduous woodland, with a small scattered Mesolithic population still practising a hunting-gathering way of life. How did agriculture make the jump?

Most experts assume that colonisation was responsible, or largely responsible, by means of a movement of experienced farmers, probably in small numbers, into the islands. Some argue strongly instead for adoption, not only using the theory of dissemination of ideas, but also by suggesting that inhabitants of the islands visited the continent and could have returned supplied with information, animals, and equipment. As the population was still very sparse, there is no reason to suppose that any newcomers were sufficiently numerous or aggressive to exterminate the indigenous inhabitants.

Groups of hunters, skilled in tracking and spearwork, might rather be expected to attack agrarian settlers who encroached on their territory. But the amount of resistance any colonists may have encountered is unknown. Evidence of intercommunal violence comes from later in the Neolithic period. It may be that initially the differences between new arrivals and established inhabitants were not very great. The earliest farmers were still hunter–gatherers: communities who lived mostly by hunting-gathering might already have embarked on some control of natural processes, like cutting and burning to make clearings, or coppicing willows to obtain wood for weaving into fish traps.

A mixed economy could have been maintained through numerous generations, with the agricultural component gradually becoming greater. Farming was a more reliable, as well as more plentiful source of food. Despite the possibilities of crop disease and animal plagues, the farmer could be more confident than the hunter about where the next meal was coming from. Considering these matters, the archaeologists, Lloyd and Jennifer Laing, suggest that the new techniques were not wholly for the better:

' . . . the advent of farming did not necessarily bring about a marked improvement in the standard of life. The hunting and gathering communities were almost certainly skilled specialists who had adapted their lifestyle to a particular economy and worked it out to a fine art.'

Some other disadvantages suggested by the Laings – like the appearance of toothache as a result of cereals in the diet, or that 'with a more assured food supply due to farming, the infirm are more likely to survive, natural selection is upset and genetic defects can be passed on more readily' – would probably not have been apparent at the time. The latter point is in any case highly speculative: there is no evidence at all of how the infirm were dealt with. But it is likely that the brief life expectancy of the hunter-gatherer, and the fertility period of women, were lengthened by the more settled life of the farmer, and this prolongation of life must have been regarded as a benefit. Indeed, the whole process is likely to have been seen as positive, and it is only a modern viewpoint, affected by such concepts as the 'noble savage' and the artificiality of modern society, that could view the domestic and social changes of the early Neolithic period as anything other than positive.

Compared with the slow-changing society of the previous millennia, the advent of farming seems almost a revolutionary development, though in fact more than 1000 years elapsed between the first patches of cultivation and the establishment throughout the islands of an agricultural way of life. In the course of that period, sheep, goats, pigs, and cows were introduced, and dogs were tamed and bred. The dramatic nature of the difference between this and previous eras is enhanced by the appearance of other technologies. Ceramic pottery began to be made. The weaving of cloth began. The range of tools and implements, though still using stone and bone for points and cutting edges, increased greatly. In flint mines and axe workshops, the beginnings of industrial process can be seen.

Just as significant were the changes in social organisation and social perception. For a Mesolithic social group, the basic criterion of life was survival from year to year. Good fortune and good weather might make some years better than others, and gradual improvement in weapon-making made hunting more efficient. But possessions were a trouble to forest nomads, and must have been kept to a minimum. For a settled Neolithic social group, it was possible to look beyond the hand-to-mouth business of survival from one year to the next. It could accumulate possessions. The extent of these possessions could be compared with those of other groups. The criteria of comfort began to improve. A certain amount of planning for the future was needed. The frequency of childbirth could be greater, and methods of child-rearing in a static community were different.

New concepts of power and ownership began to arise and a new vocabulary was needed to express them. It is possible to see that the view of nature and the universe taken by a Neolithic community could be very different from that of its own ancestors and to that of any still-Mesolithic neighbours. Yet all this was happening in a very slow and gradual fashion. Communities were not yet permanent; farming was still at a primitive level, and the scraped earth soon lost its fertility and new fields had to be made.

The effect on language must have been considerable, not only in terms of a much-expanded vocabulary but also, perhaps, in the structure and general form. Words and speech forms were a necessary and inevitable import along with new ideas and techniques, a process we are still familiar with. Along with such imported words as *sputnik* and expressions like *batterie de cuisine*, we get new coinages emerging within the language, like *floppy disk* or *E-mail*. But the process went further. The language or, more probably, languages, of the Mesolithic era were gradually abandoned in favour of a new language or, again probably, various related forms or dialects of a new language. There was more than one reason for this. Some of the islanders may have found it necessary to learn the language spoken on the continent, in order to trade and to make the kind of gift and cultural exchanges necessary to support a trading relationship. Religious and cult ideas, expressed in the continental language, may have accompanied the new technology, as an essential aspect of making it work properly. The old language might have been difficult to adapt to the more complex forms of social life being developed in the early Neolithic period. The new language may have served as a deliberate differentiation between a settled 'modern' community and an old-style nomadic one. It is not possible to give a complete and authoritative answer to this question. What we do know, however, is that it is not necessary to assume either invasion or conquest to explain a language change. In this case, it is much more likely to have been a slow cultural change, with a lengthy period of bilinguality and perhaps much transference of vocabulary and other elements, including sounds, rhythms, and accentuations, of the old language into the new one. The new language was an Indo-European one and, almost certainly, a precursor of the family of related languages that would be much later denoted as the Celtic group. Such an early use of proto-Celtic speech in the British archipelago was hardly considered by linguistic historians or archaeologists until the last two decades of the 20th century. This is partly because the first traceable uses of a 'Common Celtic' are found very much later, around 500BCE, but chiefly because of the now discarded notion that the 'Celts' had invaded the islands at some point in the first millennium BCE, bringing their language at the same time. Of the 'Celtic' traits that were taken to typify the islanders, that of language is the first and oldest. Though later differences emerged within the Celtic language group, there was a ground of basic resemblance between those languages spoken on the continent of Europe and those spoken in the British Isles. The process has been summarised by Colin Renfrew:

> 'Just as in archaeology we have come to reject both dominance models and models of complete independence in favour of interaction models, so in historical linguistics we may perhaps think of a whole language area, like the one where early Celtic was originally spoken, moving in some senses together. So that, while there would, all the time, be processes at work serving to separate out the individual dialects, yet simultaneously there would be others keeping them to some extent together, while nonetheless distinguishing them progressively from languages and dialects in other language groups, such as Italic or Germanic.'

One or two Celtic scholars have hazarded the thought that the Celtic tongues actually originated in the west, probably in Ireland, and spread from there eastwards. Neolithic Ireland was a territory of rich culture, as seen in its great burial sites and in its possession of gold; it was far from being a backward area that could only be classed as a recipient cultural zone, living off the intellectual fruits of more advanced societies. It is easier to find negative evidence than it is to prove the theory, however. The Celtic languages clearly fit into the Indo-European family, sharing a range of very basic words, which includes the numerals and many family and domestic terms, in a way that would be most improbable if they had originated at the western extreme of the continent. What is less improbable – though equally unproven – is that changes in the proto-Celtic speech arose in Ireland and spread back into Britain and Europe.

There are many unanswered and probably unanswerable questions relating to the early history of the Celtic languages, but the general outline given here seems to represent best what is known and also what fits with the evidence both of archaeology and of linguistic theory. We will return again to the matter of language in the prehistoric and historical periods but, in terms of exploring the continuity of the prehistoric population and of the ancient history of these lands, the early beginning of Celtic speech helps us to set our perspective, to appreciate that the links with the Stone Age are quite direct ones, and to realise that, in terms of speech, the British Isles probably became 'Celtic' much earlier than had once been supposed.

Early farming was a demanding business and required a great deal of work. Sufficient ground had to be cleared of trees or stones and then prepared with the use of primitive hand-held instruments. Provision had to be made for the safe storage of seed. The growing crops had to be protected from birds and animals and kept free of weeds. Harvesting, though its successful outcome must have been a feasting time from the beginning, also marked the start of a whole set of new processes. Grinding, milling, and pounding were laborious tasks, essential before foodstuffs could be produced from cereal crops, and they needed specialised equipment. But, if there were groups who clung to the older lifestyle, keeping on the move, finding food as they went along, shunning the patient toil of the farmers, it was nevertheless the farmers whose society survived.

The impact of these larger communities on the landscape was very great. The cutting and burning of woodland created large open spaces. Scrub and bushes grew where the ground was not cultivated, or where fields had been abandoned – though the concept of fertility was well understood, the process of soil fertilisation was not yet known. Their houses, barns, fences, and other structures were almost all of wood and have perished. To trace and analyse Neolithic communal sites is a complex and specialised task. The best-preserved Neolithic houses are the stone dwellings in the Orkney Islands: the two oval houses at Knap of Howar on Westray, dating back to 3600–3100BCE, and the somewhat later Skara Brae settlement, from 3100–2500BCE. In the Somerset Levels of England and the Corlea Bog in Ireland, among other locations, remains of wooden boardwalk paths have been found, of excellent carpentry workmanship, and clearly intended to provide dry passage from houses to fields and between groups of houses. They remind us that the Stone Age was also very much a Wood Age. But the most distinctive change was the commencement of building large stone structures. These began with 'causewayed enclosures' – ditched and banked open spaces with broad gaps, presumably for access, in several places round the circumference. They have been described as 'of extraordinary importance, for they represent the earliest form of non-funerary monument and the first instance of artificial enclosure of open space in the British Isles (Oswald, Dyer, and Barber, *The Creation of Monuments: Neolithic Causewayed Enclosures in the British Isles*). Their purpose or purposes can only be guessed at though, in a still-forested landscape, they evidently fulfilled the function of a meeting place. Often set on elevated sites, they were later absorbed into hillforts in most cases. In *Neolithic Britain and Ireland*, Caroline Malone writes that:

> 'At all stages in the Neolithic it seems clear that the creation of artificial open space was a preoccupation that engaged local populations in vast collective building projects lasting centuries.'

Among such constructions were the long, broad, linear cleared spaces known as *cursuses*, some of them several kilometres in length and from 20m to over 100m (66ft to over 330ft) wide. The cursus seems to have been a typically insular feature, found in Britain and Ireland, but not on the continent.

To modern eyes, just as to the 18th-century antiquarians, the most striking survivals of the Neolithic are the tombs. The houses of the dead were far grander than those of the living. From the fifth millennium BCE, along the length of what has been called the 'Atlantic façade', from Spain to Scandinavia, stone tombs were built, beginning with long barrows, earthen and turfed mounds raised over a timber or timber-and-stone inner burial chamber. Archaeologists have interpreted these as evidence of more than a new cult of the dead or religious ritual: they are seen as deliberate markers of ownership and establishment, in what was perhaps increasingly well-populated territory. However plausible, this remains a supposition. Later, round barrows became more frequent. In areas with suitable rock formations, the stone tomb was developed, its description of 'megalithic' simply meaning 'large stone'. The dolmens of Cornwall and elsewhere, now rising in sculptural form above the ground, were originally doorways to a burial chamber hidden under a great mound of earth and rubble. Much more elaborate were the great 'passage graves'. These are found mostly in mid- and northern Ireland and in northern Scotland and the northern isles, with rarer examples on Scilly and in west Wales. Though the worst temptation of the analyst of ancient cultures is to make assumptions and links from uncertain and insufficient evidence, it is thought-provoking that, in the tomb stalls and chambers of Orkney, animal remains also appear to have been buried, suggesting a symbolic connection or animal totem for a social group. Linguistic evidence relating to a much later period also hints at the same thing, with the Gaelic name of Shetland as *Innse Cat*, the cat people's islands. The great passage graves of Maes Howe on Orkney and at Knowth and Newgrange in Ireland show a combination of architectural skill, astronomical observation, and social wealth, that is far removed from the simpler structures of 2000 years previously.

But the ability of the Neolithic inhabitants to imagine, calculate, and construct on a grand scale is best seen in the many henges and stone circles which they erected. If Stonehenge in southern England is the best known, Callanish on Lewis, Brodgar and Stenness in Orkney, are also deeply impressive. Construction, alteration, and elaboration went on through the whole Neolithic era and in some cases into the Bronze Age, which followed. The formation of a whole landscape area into a ceremonial complex of circles, avenues, and perhaps water features also, shows a society with well-developed ideas about its place in the universe. Henge monuments, like the cursus, appear to be restricted to the British Isles, suggesting that, apart from the shared and transmitted ideas of the Atlantic façade, there was always a strong and creative local tradition.

The emphasis has been on objects of stone and bone, partly because few wooden artefacts have survived, but wood had a host of uses, from large-scale construction in house-building and the the hollowing-out of multiperson dugout boats, to a wide range of smaller items, such as clubs, handles, bowls, and dishes, and toggles to secure garments. It was also used to create cult objects. Tools, though diverse and specialised, were still of stone, wood, and bone. But knowledge of basic mechanics already existed. Writing of the construction of Stonehenge, Lloyd and Jennifer Laing note that there is 'no concrete reason for believing that the builders of Stonehenge were not in possession of the wheel, and it is not impossible that they had pulleys.' Solid wooden wheels dating back to around 2500BCE have been found in the Netherlands.

In the two millennia of the Neolithic, the population of the islands grew substantially from its early small base. Evidence of this is clear from the increasing number of inhabited sites and their greater area. In addition, the monumental structures put up in this era required increasingly great numbers of man-hours in their construction. Even allowing for slow progress, such building can only have been possible when the population was large enough to provide a supply of able-bodied persons as builders, in addition to those who worked on herding, woodcutting, tool-making, food production, and preparation. Perhaps slaves formed a part of the workforce. Although it may be that many Neolithic sites have been destroyed beyond recognition, it seems apparent from what we can see that the present imbalance of population between south and north was not the case in the Neolithic period. The Shetland Islands, for example, show a high concentration of Neolithic sites. Allowing for a higher likelihood of preservation there, it is still a striking example of how the early population had spread across the entire land area. It may also offer a hint – if an element of immigration is allowed for – that some of those people had come from the northeast of the continent, migrating south rather than northwards. It should also be noted, though, that, around 3000–1500BCE, the regional climate was both warmer and drier than it later became.

CHAPTER THREE

Metal Users

'Once arrived, these several waves of energetic conquerors soon occupied the greater part of Britain, ruthlessly dispossessing the Neolithic communities of their best pastures, and also no doubt of their herds, and sometimes of their women.'

This quotation from Jacquetta and Christopher Hawkes's *Prehistoric Britain* calls to mind Malcolm Chapman's comment that some writers seem to have toured the prehistoric world with camera and tape recorder. It describes the supposed arrival of the pottery-making battle-axe-collecting 'Beaker Folk' at the beginning of the Bronze Age, around 2750BCE. It must be said that Christopher Hawkes later greatly diluted his robustly-described 'invasion' theory in favour of a gradual process which he called 'cumulative Celticity'. What, then, of those round 'Beaker folk' skulls, which earlier archaeologists set so much store by? Their discovery in the new-type round barrow grave sites was said to mark a racial difference from the 'long-headed skulls' of the earlier Neolithic inhabitants. But the number of examples was very small and their one-time prominence shows the danger of seizing on limited evidence to draw large conclusions. In the later 20th century, the focus of exploration of the prehistoric periods moved away from actual human remains, of which few examples were to hand, to the evidence of social life, of which much more evidence was being found, due to photographic, biological, chemical, and radiation-based research techniques. There was also a certain reluctance, following the excesses of the Nazi period in Germany and Austria, to make any sort of generalisation with regard to race. More importantly, the evidence of excavated sites shows no sign of sudden dramatic change at this time. Once again, continuity, and innovation within continuity, is revealed. Lloyd and Jennifer Laing, while adhering to the migration theory, accept that 'the Beaker folk mixed easily and peacefully with the native inhabitants'. In most sites of the period, there is a mingling of new 'Beaker' styles and artefacts with the old Neolithic tradition.

The Beaker Folk no longer loom as large as they once did in accounts of the transition to the use of copper, and then bronze, tools and utensils. But the transition certainly took place, and some experts still opt for a combination of limited immigration and the islanders' imitation of 'prestige' items from the continent. James Dyer offers an interesting suggestion relating to the new fashion for shaped and decorated drinking vessels:

> 'It is conceivable that these vessels may have been no more than the appropriate accompaniment to a new drink that swept the country – mead, barley or fruit wine, or even something with hallucinatory powers.'

But new pottery styles were only part of the development. Changes and variations in burial procedures suggest that cultural shifts were taking place – we are still looking at a timescale of generations here – and it is likely that the overall pattern of societies and customs within the islands was far from uniform. In the round barrows and ring cairns of the transitional era, some bodies were cremated – the corpse already partly desiccated by exposure to the open air – before interment; some were not. Some tombs were found to hold examples of both methods. It was around 1500BCE before cremation seems to have become the usual, though not the universal, process of burial. But, with the advent of 'Beaker' designs, a trend away from the collective graves of earlier times is apparent, and single graves, often under a low mound, are found, in which the body lies accompanied by a beaker, perhaps originally filled with a liquor of some kind, together with arrowheads, a copper dagger, a wristguard of stone, and perhaps a few personal ornaments of bone or amber, or even gold. Such a person is inevitably, and not unreasonably considered to be a 'warrior' or 'chief': a high-status figure whose superiority is accepted by the rest of the community. The graves of high-status females have no weapons, but similar beakers and ornaments. Other graves in the proximity of such a one often have no goods in them at all, suggesting a lower status as retainers.

Not everyone died a natural death. Communities were impinging on one another, and not always peacefully. Evidence of social violence goes back into the Neolithic period. Causewayed enclosures in Devon, Cornwall, and elsewhere show, by scattered arrowheads and evidence of wooden palisades destroyed by fire, that they had been attacked. At Hambledon Hill, in Dorset, the remains of a body were found in the ditch, the arrowhead that killed it still in its chest. Warfare was clearly an element in social life. By 1600BCE, there is widespread evidence of offensive weapons and their use. Other than that warfare on a local scale existed, it is hard to draw any real inferences from this. Attacks, battles, weapon-making imply both certain forms of social organisation and a set of attitudes about other communities. The role of chiefs or war leaders may be surmised, but nothing can be established with definition or even probability.

Skulls from this period also sometimes show evidence of trepanning, with holes drilled through the bone. In some cases, this may have been the cause of death but, in others, the trepanning had long preceded death. The purpose has generally been taken to be medicinal, although some writers have suggested that shamanic practices, as known from later Siberian cultures, might underlie it. Though some kind of cult reason is perfectly possible – medicine and ritual would have been inextricably combined – there is no evidence to link these practices, associated with distant subarctic peoples, to the religious observations of the Celtic-speaking peoples. The 'shamanistic' verses attributed to bards like Taliesin come from a period more than 1000 years later, and savour more of being a quite sophisticated literary device than of being primitive spell texts.

Through the Bronze Age and into that of Iron, there is increasing evidence of weapon-making. The population was continuing to grow, which might suggest both a larger number of people involved in warfare and also more opportunities to indulge in it. It also seems that the social importance of the warrior was growing as his equipment became more elaborate and effective. The 'arms race' as a driver of technical progress dates from here if not earlier. But many Bronze- and Iron-Age sites show no sign of defensive walling. Typical isolated farmsteads like that at Little Woodbury, in Wiltshire, had fences that served to keep tame animals in and wild animals out, but which would not have held off a human enemy force.

In Ireland and in Britain, the later Bronze Age was a time of prosperity and social expansion. Copper deposits in southwest Ireland were exploited from early in the second millennium BCE, and shafts sunk around 1500–1250BCE have been explored at Mount Gabriel, near Schull, in County Cork. Ireland was also an important source of gold, already long well known, accepted and sought for as the most valuable of metals; ownership or control of a gold source, and of the subsequent working of the metal, was undoubtedly a matter of high prestige. There is much fine goldwork of the period in Ireland. In *Pre-Christian Ireland*, Peter Harbison notes that:

'Together with the [bronze] horns and cauldrons, the greatest glory of Ireland's Late Bronze Age is undoubtedly its gold-work.'

The torcs, necklaces, and ornaments indicate the existence of a social level at which the possession and display of wealth was customary. It would naturally follow that cultural and social influences should spread from such an area. Equally, the arrival of visitors coming to trade would bring in new ideas.

Transport was improving. Horses, long kept as draught animals, began to be ridden in the Bronze Age, and many examples of finely made harness rings and bits have been found.

Bronze-Age rock drawings in Norway show boats rowed by as many as 50 men and, though nothing similar has been found in the British Isles, the existence of such large vessels would help to explain the movement of large heavy objects like the monolithic bluestones of Stonehenge, from the Preseli and Snowdon mountains of Wales. Long-distance routeways, at first concerned with the carriage of salt and of flints, and later of metal, were long established. The presence on many sites of stone axes, some of them clearly ceremonial in purpose, including imported ones of jade, suggest that these artefacts had a special importance, in trading or gift exchange, or in ritual use, or all of these. 'Trading routes' at this time need not imply that a producer at one end was consigning a shipment to some specific person at the other end, or somewhere on the line. Rather, goods found their own way along the route, traded and exchanged from one area to another, in sufficient quantity, presumably, to satisfy demand at all points. It might well have taken a single item many years to traverse the whole route.

Anticipating the later medieval cathedrals that have undergone great extension and rebuilding, as well as certain changes in the cult, over their centuries-long history, Stonehenge, over a period of 1700 years from the Mesolithic to the Bronze Age, underwent great changes, evolving from a simple henge – an open circular area surrounded by a ditch and an external bank – to the complex and massive structure of later times. Henges date from around 2500BCE and seem to have replaced the earlier causewayed enclosures. While Stonehenge has unique aspects, its history of development was paralleled by other monuments. The alignment has long been noted: from the construction period of around 2000BCE, it faced, in one direction, the midsummer sunrise and, in the other, the midwinter sunset, while the long side of the rectangle formed by the four 'station stones' indicate the most southerly rising and most northerly setting of the moon. The astronomical orientation of this and other monuments is clear, though the nature of the cult is not.

In the same Wessex region, at the same time as the final phases of construction at Stonehenge, around 1800–1400BCE, there is evidence of a rich upper stratum of society, found in a number of grave sites. The occupants of these graves – some are also found elsewhere in southern England – were clearly people of wealth and status. Far exceeding the quality and value of any other grave goods of the era in the British Isles, the contents include gold ornaments and fine copper- and bronzework. They also include many imported items, including faïence beads from Europe (some archaeologists have suggested Egypt as the ultimate source) and objects fashioned of amber, whose main source was the Baltic coasts. None of these materials was local to Wessex, whose chalk downlands provided fertile soil and pasture, but their presence as possessions suggests considerable trading power. What the Wessex chiefs had to offer in return is not known. Their area may have been a creative centre where Irish gold and Baltic amber were formed by craftspeople into desirable items: an amber necklace was found in a grave shaft at Mycenae. At this time the Minoan-Mycenaean culture of the eastern Mediterranean was at a high point, and it is perfectly feasible to suppose a long slow passage route by which goods from either end of the road could be passed, via many middlemen, from one end to the other by the process of exchange.

With the sea in use as a highway as well as a great food resource, a large proportion of the population was then distributed along the coasts. The British archipelago, placed on the great arc linking the Iberian and Armorican peninsulas and the coastline of northern Europe, may have been a central location on an important southwest-to-northeast axis of trade and exchange. The Great Glen of Scotland offered a valuable portage route between the northern and the western seas, avoiding the tide races of the Pentland Firth and the storms of the Minch, whose legends of the ship-devouring 'Blue Men' are probably very ancient indeed. Travellers by sea did not go far from land, and beached their small vessels at night. Cultural influences from both directions met in the middle areas and brought the enrichment of news and novelties, but the travellers also acquired information and observed rites and methods in the places where they stayed, and took this away with them. Rather than being at the back of beyond – as they later seemed to the Romans – in the Atlantic context, early British communities may have been at the centre of things, with a consequent energy, creativity, and dynamism in all aspects of life, including language and religion.

Some language historians have felt there are reasons to attribute the beginnings of Celtic language in the British Isles to the period of cultural change that marked the beginnings of the Bronze Age. The Irish philologist, Myles Dillon, noted how features of the 'Wessex Culture' seemed to correspond to the warrior aristocracy that is depicted in the Irish legends. He could see no reason why a cultural and linguistic tradition should not have arisen from this period onwards. We might note, however, that the Wessex burials appear to have been exceptional in the British Isles.

CHAPTER FOUR

Iron Users – the Celts Enter History

With the gradual advent and improvement of iron tools, general standards of living may have improved. Unlike bronze, which was quite rare, and tin, which was even rarer and, therefore, also very expensive, iron was quite widely available, easier to work, and so cheaper to buy. But, from late in the second millennium BCE, environmental conditions were worsening. A gradual steady change in the weather pattern brought cooler wetter weather to the British archipelago, with occasional very hard winters. Upland and island communities were most seriously affected. Dartmoor, a well-populated area in the earlier Bronze Age, with farmsteads up to 450m (1500ft), compared with the present-day maximum of 300m (1000ft), became increasingly inhospitable and many sites were abandoned. Forests on mountain ranges like the Cairngorms and Mournes died away (the stumps of great pines can still be seen). Internal migrations, no doubt, led to social tensions as sheltered and fertile ground became of greater worth. The climatic change encouraged the growth of peat and the spread of marshy areas. By 1500BCE, the 'Neoglacial' epoch was well established. The effects of this were severe in Scandinavia – H. H. Lamb suggests, in *Climate History and the Modern World*, that from this era arose the later legend of the dreaded, murderously cold *fimbulwinter*, which may have encouraged some southward population movement into the British islands. From around 900BCE, new wooden trackways were being built in the Somerset Levels, to counter a rise in the water level but, by 350, the inhabitants often had to use boats. Between 800BCE and 400BCE, the bogland at Tregaron, in west Wales, increased by a metre in thickness – it took the next 2000 years to achieve a similar degree of increase.

Hillforts with walls and ditches date from the later Middle Bronze Age, around 1200BCE, and became increasingly common from around 900. Such developments were once assumed to be the responses to invasive movements from Europe, the last ripples of a vast turmoil among peoples far to the east and south caused by the breakdown of the Minoan-Mycenaean civilisation of the eastern Mediterranean area. Although the earliest hillforts were built in southern England, this was a region of relatively dense population, and they can equally well be explained by internal strife and competition. Peaceful uses, as sites of manufacture or exchange, have also been suggested, especially as many hillforts have shown little or no evidence of inhabitation. Although, particularly in Alpine Europe, the colder weather was displacing hill-dwelling peoples, it cannot be supposed that the oceanic islands offered a particularly desirable refuge.

Between 900 and 700BCE new metalworking techniques were being introduced into the islands. As bronzework reached its highest point in weapons, tools, and ornament, the use of iron, a metal of greater effectiveness in the first two roles, was becoming known. It did not totally displace bronze, or bone, or even stone implements. The great and continuing advantage of the two latter was that they were anciently familiar, and more readily available. People could make their own tools with them, and their use continued into the Common Era. Both iron- and bronzeworking were specialised crafts. In the Bronze and early Iron Ages, at least, smiths were often itinerants, moving from place to place in order to provide their services. This has been established from the discovery of numerous deposits of bronze and iron, either raw ore or scrap for remaking, close to prehistoric trackways. These were left, no doubt after careful identification of the place, by smiths against their return to do further work in the locality. How a smith learned his craft is not known; the likelihood is that, most often, the knowledge was passed on within a family from father to son or uncle to nephew. While the making of implements is an essentially practical business, it is certain that, as with all other forms of human activity at that time, the actual work was intermingled with aspects of ritual and cult. In all ancient lore, the smith is a figure of power and often has magic qualities. His power is reflected back into the classical pantheon of gods and demigods, with figures such as Vulcan and Prometheus. With the control of fire, the ability to shape rough lumps of hard ore into shining and desirable objects, the sense of practising an arcane technique, the smith's prestige was extremely high. If the 'magic' aspect of his work helped to keep it a trade secret and discouraged amateur practitioners, this was a by-product rather than the prime reason. In the case of the bronzesmiths, who continued to make armour and helmets long into the Iron Age, the particular designs they worked into the surfaces would have been seen as conveying supernatural powers of strength or protection, in complement to the strength of the metal itself.

Such work required payment. Coinage was still a long way off from the British Isles in the mid-first millennium BCE. Payment was in kind, perhaps of dyed woollen cloth, or pottery items, or salt, or animals, whatever high-value goods the community itself had a surplus of. A smith would have been a wealthy man, desirable as a husband or father-in-law.

Not everything made by the smiths was for utility or ornament. Many deposits of tools and weapons were made for ritual or religious reasons. This practice went on for centuries and it is quite probable that the underlying ideas changed or evolved or were different in different localities. Some writers have suggested that, in some cases at least, the deposited articles were part of the booty secured after victory in battle. In some cases, the objects deposited were broken, apparently before being deposited, as a deliberate practice, rather than simply being dumped as unusable. In other cases, swords and shields have been recovered that were clearly made specially as cere-monial objects, not for practical use. In other cases, entire usable weapons have been found. There would have been nothing random about the selection of items for this purpose, or about the choice of location. Water almost always seems to have played an important part in these practices – a theme to be revisited when we encounter the 'historical Celts'.

As the use of iron was spreading in Ireland and Britain, there were significant developments happening a few hundred miles away in central Europe. From around 750BCE, what has become known as the 'Hallstatt culture' becomes evident. Hallstatt itself is located in the Austrian Alps and its rise to wealth over a period of several hundred years is owed prima-rily to the digging-out and export of extensive rock-salt deposits and, secondarily, to its position in central Europe with north–south and east–west connections via mountain passes and great river valleys, which enabled the passage of raw mate-rials, manufactured objects, and, importantly, knowledge.

The Hallstatt culture itself developed from the Bronze-Age 'Urnfield' culture of a wide area of central Europe, so-called from a number of apparently related social customs, including the burial of cremated remains in assemblages of decorative urns. The importance of this in Celtic studies lies in the accep-tance by authoritative scholars that the continental Celtic lan-guage here took on the form that was then maintained into the historical period. Professor Barry Cunliffe, in a new introduc-tory chapter (1997) to Nora Chadwick's *The Celts*, writes:

'If we are correct that the Celtic language crystallised among the Late Bronze Age Urnfield communities of Middle Europe, the extensive links which must have existed with Atlantic

Europe at this time would have provided a context for Celtic to have been widely adopted as a *lingua franca*, accompanying the flow of goods and technological information.'

The 'if' at the beginning should not be ignored; Cunliffe is suggesting what, to him as a leading archaeologist, is an attractive and perfectly reasonable hypothesis. But the linguistic homology between central and Atlantic Europe could have already existed. Exchange and trade between these regions began earlier than the Late Bronze Age.

Hallstatt was a focus of technical innovation and of adaptations from neighbouring peoples. The spoked and iron-tyred wheel, and a new type of slashing sword have both been identified with it, and both would have been eagerly imitated. The Hallstatt culture, from the earlier Iron Age (it is now identified in four separate stages, between the eighth and fifth centuries BCE) has had less visible impact upon insular sites, although its development of ironworking methods must have been of great importance. From around 500BCE, however, its importance declined, but there remained, or developed, other European sites of great wealth, identified with the presence of chieftain-led societies, which had a culture of display and a wealthy aristocratic element to indulge in it. These have been collectively identified as the 'La Tène culture', from a site at the edge of Lake Neuchâtel, in present-day Switzerland. La Tène itself appears to have been an important ritual place, where offerings were placed in the waters of the lake, and a wide range of objects has been recovered from here. Beginning in the mid-fifth century, it lasted until the Roman conquest of Gaul, towards the end of the last century BCE. The region where the La Tène culture arose, straddling the north-south route between northern Europe and the Mediterranean, had definite trading contacts with the British Isles. Its influence there has been seen in the construction method of hillforts, as well as in much of the 'insular' artistic design practised in later centuries.

Hallstatt and La Tène form the two acknowledged high points of Celtic art before the later eras of island metalwork, of the Pictish sculptured stones, and of the Irish and Scottish manuscript books and carved high crosses. Celtic scholars are agreed that the influence of La Tène, in particular, was strong on what is known as 'insular' Celtic art, i.e. that of the British Isles, where it is most clearly seen in metalwork. The origins of the typical semiabstract swirling designs and motifs found on scabbards, brooches, shields, and harness fittings, which later influenced manuscript illustration and stone-carving, are often dated to the La Tène period, though this question is further discussed in Chapter Fourteen.

After our long delving among the roots of the peoples of the islands, it is finally at this time, around 500BCE, that specific historical reference to Celts can be found – though not in connection with the British Isles. Greek writers begin to refer to the *Keltoi* as a European people or group of peoples. At the beginning of the fifth century, Hecataeus, among the earliest Greek historians, refers to the Greek colony of Massilia (Marseilles) as being founded 'in the land of Ligurians near the lands of the Celts'. This is the first recorded mention of Celts. Herodotus, at much the same time, states that the River Danube rises in the land of the Celts, near the town of Pyrene. This town has not been traced and some scholars think it means the Pyrenees. Thus begins a long tradition of confused, brief, and often ambiguous comments from Greek and Roman sources on the Celts. Elsewhere in his writing, Herodotus refers to the Celts as the most westerly people of Europe, apart from the Cynesii, who lived on the Atlantic coast of Iberia. At this time, the remoter Atlantic coasts and islands, though known to Greek and other Mediterranean traders, hardly impinged on the consciousness of the civilised world. An early source from around 600BCE, lost but surviving in later references, is known as the *Massiliot Periplus*, or 'Marseilles Journey-book', a sailing manual. It describes Atlantic islands known as the Oestrymnides, with tin and lead mines, at two days' sailing distance from Ireland, and inhabited by a vigorous people, who used boats made of sewn hides. A reference to their well-populated ridges suggests they were large islands, but their identity is not clear. The account of the traveller, Pytheas of Marseilles, from around 330BCE, is first to mention the name of the 'Prettanic Isles', later rendered as 'Britannic'. His text was tucked away in the great Library at Alexandria, and lost or destroyed; and it also is only known from partial later transcripts. The name 'Prettanic' has led the French scholar, Henri Hubert, to the opinion that 'it is derived from the name of the Picts (*Pretanni, Prydain*), the Celtic origin of which is doubted'. But it is also possible that this name, *Prydein* in Brittonic, *Cruithne* in Gaelic, was given to the Picts by their neighbours. Its meaning is not known.

In the course of the next two centuries, Greeks and Romans became uncomfortably aware of the Celts. From their population centres in middle and east central Europe, the tribal groups spread southwards in large numbers, in different assemblages, at different times, impelled by forces of which we know nothing, and apparently looking for territory to settle in. The fact that they were organised for warfare means that either they knew it would have to be by conquest or they hoped to gather up booty on the way. In 390BCE, they emerged into high prominence by successfully attacking no less a place than Rome. The city, already the most powerful in Italy, was looted and the invaders, of the Senones tribe led by Brennus, were eventually bought off by a large payment of gold. Other invading tribes were also given Latinised names by the Romans, the Insubres, the Cenomani, the Boii, and the Lingones. Though references have been made in some popular books to a 'Celtic empire', they were not organised as an empire, or even as a confederacy; their invasions were independent expeditions made over a period of nearly 200 years. A hundred years after the sack of Rome, a wandering warlike group of Celtic-speakers, called Galatians by the Greeks, searching for a homeland in eastern Europe, but also taking opportunistic chances to terrorise and plunder, defeated the once-invincible Macedonians. In 279BCE, another group of Galatians, led by another Brennus, pushed far into Greece and raided the shrine of the Oracle at Delphi. Eventually, by an accommodation with the local ruler, they found a homeland in central Anatolia and settled there, to become the Christian Galatians, whom St Paul had cause to reprove. The European expansion of the Celts – or of peoples speaking a Celtic language and of similar cultural and social characteristics – is relatively well documented. By the first century BCE, a huge swathe of the continent, from the Iberian peninsula to Thrace and on into Asia Minor, was inhabited largely by Celtic peoples.

From a later insular point of view, one of these peoples or population groups, the Celtiberians, are of particular interest. The area now known as Spain and Portugal had an aboriginal population that, as far as anyone knows, goes back to the earliest days of *Homo sapiens sapiens* in western Europe. From the Late Bronze Age, inland and to the north, there appear to have been strong cultural and linguistic affinities with the 'Urnfield' inhabitants on the north side of the Pyrenees, resulting in the development of what Greeks and Romans could recognise as a 'Celtic' society. They distinguished between 'Celts' and 'Iberians' but, by the second century, the term Celtiberian had been coined, to imply a fusion or union of peoples: it is not a linguistic term. The Iberians are assumed to have spoken non-Indo-European languages, of which Basque was one; the Celtiberians spoke a Celtic language, though it may have had Iberian elements. On the eastern Mediterranean coast, a strong Carthaginian influence was installed from the late second century. Outside the zone of Carthaginian control, the Celtiberians were culturally and, it would seem, also militarily, dominant, and a process of Celticisation extended west and south in the peninsula. But, in the course of bloody and protracted warfare through most of the second century, the entire vast region became a Roman province, Hispania. As with the Roman provinces of Gaul, the Celtic language or languages were then progressively ousted by new language forms based on Latin. Of the possibly numerous pre-Indo-European, and thus pre-Celtic, languages of western Europe, the only modern survivor is Basque.

Archaeologists and prehistorians have identified links along what Barry Cunliffe has evocatively called 'the Atlantic façade', which go back centuries before the Roman invasions, at least as far as the Neolithic. The passage graves of Portugal and Ireland are taken as evidence of some shared culture, and Bronze-Age shipwrecks have been found off the British southern coast, carrying French-made artefacts. However sporadic and slight, the contacts were maintained over a very lengthy period and, with the greater demand for tin in the Late Bronze Age, may have intensified around that time, with greater exploitation of the trade routes, leading to more frequent and meaningful interchange. As we will see when we look at the legendary origins of the people of Ireland, there is a strong tradition of links with Spain. However, the actual evidence for links between the Celtic speakers of the Iberian peninsula and the inhabitants of Hibernia is very slight. It is improbable that navigators braved the wide and stormy gulf of the Bay of Biscay. Prehistoric sailors preferred to skirt the coast and to anchor or beach their vessels overnight. The passage of goods, people, and ideas is likely to have been in a series of daily journeys, or by transfer to new carriers at certain points.

The continental tribes, all speaking a version of Common Celtic, had less connection with the inhabitants of the British Isles than they did with the Italic and Greek peoples whom they invaded. 'Celt' was a convenient label for a group of peoples whom the Greeks, and, later, the Romans neither understood nor wished to understand. They were barbarians and enemies. In a similar way, 'Scythian' was used for the peoples north of the Celts; these were terms as broad as present-day 'Asiatic', showing nothing more than a highly generalised geographical presence. In the days when language dissemination and the process of 'acculturation' could only be explained by large-scale population movements and invasions, it was felt essential to show that the Celts had come from somewhere. That convenient vague location, of vast extent and lacking any precise boundaries, the southern steppes of Russia, was accepted. The Celtic peoples had emerged from there and spread westwards during the first millennium BCE. How or why was not seriously examined, nor was what happened to the already well-established populations. The original Celts, if such a group existed, did not emerge from the region of the first farmers, which lay further south than the Steppes, in a zone whose ancient languages are known to have been not Celtic but Indo-Aryan and Semitic. It is far more logical to accept that the Celtic forms of speech and other manifestations of what could be called Celtic culture arose among and were adopted by the already-established inhabitants of central and western Europe.

But, as there is considerable historical evidence of large-scale migration, invasion, and warfare associated with Celtic peoples in southern Europe, it is reasonable to ask, What of the islands? Did war bands or colonists cross the water, from eastwards or the south, or both? Was this the time – from 500BCE on – that a Celtic aristocracy, with superior iron-based technology, established its power over the indigenous islanders?

Such was the assumption of scholars from the 18th century until far into the 20th, and many people still accept it. But, if there were invasions at that time, there is remarkably little evidence of them. Since the islands were not yet of concern to Greek or Roman historians and the continental Celts only of interest insofar as they impinged on the Greeks and Romans, one would not expect a written record. The references to be gleaned from Polybius (c.202–120BCE) and Posidonius (c.135–51BCE, and known only through later borrowings from his work) are sparse and shed no light on population movement. But the intensive work of archaeologists over the past 100 years, though it often shows patterns of localised cultural changes, has not revealed traces of invasion.

In this period, the British Isles were in a state of relative decline. The long phase of cooler, wetter weather had taken hold. Barry Cunliffe notes that in Ireland 'from the beginning of the sixth century to the end of the second century BC there is little trace of any contact with continental developments, and indeed the dendrochronological [tree-ring] evidence shows that over large areas forests were regenerating – an observation suggestive of a dramatic decline in population.' It is notable that the Western Isles, around the first century BCE, in the same oceanic climate zone, were reported by the explorer, Demetrius of Tarsus, to be largely unpopulated, though there is ample archaeological evidence of human occupancy in previous centuries. During the centuries when the European Celtic migrations were at their height, from the fourth to the second BCE, there is a substantial fall in the amount of artefacts found in the British Isles that can be traced to Europe or even to European influence. From this, it is reasonable to infer that the islands and the islanders were left on their own. There cannot have been much to tempt invaders: a poor climate, few valuable resources beyond the tin mines of Cornwall, a warlike population already contesting for the most favoured soil. In the work already quoted from (*The Ancient Celts*), professor Cunliffe notes further that:

'The material culture of Atlantic Scotland is limited and indigenous in the extreme, suggesting a high degree of cultural isolation throughout most of the Iron Age [from around 700BC into the Christian era], though there is evidence of developing contact along the Atlantic seaways in and after the first century BC.'

'Material culture' means objects and artefacts and, in a number of areas, there is certainly evidence of metalwork that is inspired by or modelled on the designs found in the later Hallstatt and the La Tène deposits. From the fourth century BCE in Britain, and the third in Ireland, these form a range of items, all of a ceremonial or ritual nature. Among them are torcs (neck collars),

swords and daggers, trinkets and ornaments, and items of
harness from horses and wheeled vehicles. The most prolific
location of these is in east Yorkshire, where fourth-century
cemetery sites have been discovered, the design of their graves,
and, in a few cases, the contents, similar to the early La Tène
style. Some of these graves contained the remnants of two-
wheeled chariots or carts. Most of the other items found,
including the pottery, are clearly from the insular tradition. It
seems that in this area an elite group, who might have emerged
locally or who could have been immigrants, established a form
of rule that was deliberately modelled in some ways on the
aristocratic-warrior societies of La Tène. The lack of actual
continental-made items suggests that they were not immigrants.
It should be noted, however, that a few hundred years later, in
Roman times, the name of the tribe who inhabited this area was
given as the Parisii: a tribal name also found in Gaul in the
neighbourhood of present-day Paris. Other items showing La
Tène influence have been found elsewhere in England, mostly
in the south. The third-century Irish swords found in bog
deposits in the central lowlands show a similar influence, but
they are locally made and not imported; rather than any kind of
invasion or migration, they show what is entirely to be expected,
a continuation of age-old cultural links with the continent. In
the context of Irish history, the abandonment of the 'Invasion
Theory' is even more of a turnabout than in the British context.
Barry Raftery wrote in 1994 that 'it seems almost heretical to
insist that a Celtic invasion of Ireland never happened' (*Pagan
Celtic Ireland*), but to those concerned for their 'Celticness', a
long social, cultural, and linguistic continuity back into the
Bronze Age and earlier is surely an even more satisfactory assur-
ance of inherited identity and association with the land than a
descent from later invaders.

CHAPTER FIVE

The Islanders – Language and Social Life in the Pre-Roman Era

The ancestral forms of Gaelic, Pictish, Welsh, and the other Celtic languages have been traced back, as we have seen, to a language or perhaps a language pool comprising a range of related dialects, known as Common Celtic. This was spoken in central Europe, and perhaps in the British Isles also, from the Bronze Age and is presumed to have supplanted earlier languages. We know from our personal experience, as well as from philology, that there is nothing, and never was anything, static about language. It is constantly changing, in pronunciation, grammar, and vocabulary, to the distress of the conservatively inclined in all periods of history. In the case of Common Celtic, which was a spoken tongue only, this was even more true: writing exercises a slight brake on language's tendency to change.

There is still a great deal that is obscure, and much that is controversial or currently unprovable, as far as the timescale of Celtic language development is concerned. Colin Renfrew supposes 'an Indo-European speaking population in France and in Britain and in Ireland, and probably in much of Iberia also, by before 4000BC.' The Indo-European speech of these peoples evolved towards the Celtic languages. Not all experts would accept this, and Renfrew himself treats it as a grand generalisation. But few specialists, whether in language history, cultural history, or archaeology, would now disagree that the local roots of the Celtic languages of Britain are very much older than was once supposed.

From these mists of time we move forward to the semiclarity of the first century BCE. By mid-century, Julius Caesar had made his reconnaissance and followed up with a tentative, failed invasion of Britain. The islands and their inhabitants were much better known, though wild surmises and rumours show that there was still much ignorance, especially of Ireland. By this time, two Celtic languages, or dialect groups, are known to have been spoken in the British Isles. These are Goidelic and Brittonic. A third, Pictish, can perhaps be surmised, though its existence does not become apparent until much later. Broadly, Goidelic appears to have been the speech of Ireland, and Brittonic that of Britain. These two, with Goidelic in its Gaelic form, and Brittonic in its later forms of Welsh and Breton, are the principal Celtic languages to survive. As a result, much of the definition of the Celtic language group is dependent on them. The residual elements of the continental Celtic languages, and of Pictish, other than a few place names, are so fragmentary that it is very difficult to use them in any form of comparison. In the old scholarly view of language history, which schematised development into 'family trees', with languages stemming from a parent branch, it was supposed that Goidelic and Brittonic had split away from a Common Celtic parent. Either they had diverged as a single language, which then divided again, or they split away at different times, with Goidelic, as the more 'primitive' form, being the first to do so.

The prime evidence for this is the well known *p* and *qu* (sometimes shown as *kw* or *k*) difference between the two. In older Celtic languages, the sound qu- is echoed in other Indo-European tongues: thus Latin *quattuor*, four, is cognate with Gaelic *cethir*; and Latin *qui*, who, is cognate with Gaelic *cia*. The equivalent Welsh words are *pedwar* and *pwi*, clearly showing that the initial letter has undergone a change of sound, and, later, spelling. Similarly, Gaelic *ceann*, head, is matched by Welsh *pen*. Enough of Gaulish survives to show that it too was *p*-Celtic. The Celtic inscriptions of Iberia are very rare, and hard to read, but it seems that the speech of the Celtiberians was *qu*-Celtic (something which has excited those who hunt for Irish origins in Spain). The dating of the shift from *qu* to *p* is not clear, any more than is its locality of origin. It is generally assumed to have come about in the first millennium BCE, perhaps some time before 500BCE, and to have begun on the European continent, perhaps in Gaul. For unknown reasons it failed to reach, or to be adopted by, the remotest regions, Spain and Ireland. Hispano-Celtic perished but, in Ireland, the *qu* form produced Gaelic and Manx, while, in Britain, the *p* form developed into Brittonic and the very similar Cumbric of the North Britons, and later Cornish and Welsh.

The general picture is neat, but it contains many gaps and problems. Some of these problems are eased if we stop thinking about language development on the overschematic family-tree basis, and instead regard language as a dialect pool, in which localised changes and developments may occur and sometimes be passed on. Geographical, cultural, and economic causes might all play a part in this. Some specific problems in Celtic language history relate to the peoples known as Picts, inhabiting Scotland north of the Forth-Clyde line, whose language, despite their northern peripheral location, appears to have been a *p*-Celtic one. Language scholars working on the scanty remains of Pictish have concluded that it was not Goidelic, and that, rather than being a close relative of Brittonic, it was nearer in form to Gaulish, the Celtic language spoken in what is now France. Both Pictish and Gaulish are known only though place and personal names and inscriptions found in archaeological discoveries. The processual, or wave, theory of language spread does not readily explain how a 'later' *p*-Celtic form can exist among a people situated beyond the 'earlier' *qu*-Celtic speakers. There is no evidence to suggest that the Picts were in close trading contact with the Gaulish tribes; rather the reverse. Since the rejection of 'invasion' theories, the provenance and manner of introduction of this Pictish language have not been explored. It can be used to sustain both the 'invasion' theory – that the leading elements of Pictish society came, perhaps in the first century, from Gaul – and the 'indigenous' theory – that, in its remote region, the Pictish language did not pick up the changes that came to characterise Brittonic. A further and hotly contested issue relates to whether a pre-Celtic language was preserved among the Picts; the so-far indecipherable lettered inscriptions on a number of Pictish sculptured stones keep this question warm.

The language issue is important since, as Myles Dillon made clear, the acceptance of long residence by Celtic speakers in Ireland and Britain should mean acceptance of the view that the change in the Gaulish and Brittonic languages from *qu* to *p* happened during a period when speakers of a Celtic language were already living in Ireland. Dillon saw such speech innovations spreading from a centre on the continent and failing to reach as far as the 'lateral' areas of Ireland and Spain, where the old forms remained in use. But the Irish Cruithne are there as evidence of *p*-Celtic speakers in Ireland from early times. How did the Gaels fail to adopt this change if they lived amidst people who did? Were the Gaels, or rather proto-Gaels, somewhere else at the time? Was that somewhere else located in the Iberian peninsula (whose Celtiberian speech is considered to have been *qu*-Celtic)? Such questions remain unanswerable, at least until further concrete evidence is produced, in the form of comparable texts or word samples.

In any case, however, the general relationship of language between the islands and the continent during the last few centuries of the pre-Common Era and the first centuries CE is undeniable. This position did not last. Celtic languages on the continent had virtually disappeared from use by the end of the fourth century CE, while the 'Insular Celtic' forms of the British Isles remained and continued to evolve. But, as we have seen, this linguistic affinity does not imply that they were all one people, or had one political system, or had anything in common that could define the islanders as 'Celts'.

One of the consequences of both the 'invasion' and the 'dissemination' theories is that most archaeologists and ancient historians have regarded the British Isles peoples as recipients rather than originators. This is not only because of their peripheral location, with the sense that things ultimately wash up at the edge. Cultural remains on continental Europe are generally richer, as well as more extensive. In addition, once lines of continuity can be traced (this is not until historic 'Celtic' times), there is clear evidence of continental influence on the islanders' activities, as with the La Tène-style metal-working. However, there is evidence that the islanders also had their own ideas, practices, and techniques, whether adapted from elsewhere or completely home-grown. A notable example is that of the Scottish brochs: circular windowless dry-stone towers with low passage-style entrances; though there is some resemblance to prehistoric structures on Sardinia, they are essentially a unique building form. The Caledonians' attachment to the war chariot, which surprised the Romans at the battle of Mons Graupius in Scotland in 78CE, may be an example of insular conservatism, but it also shows that the islanders were not necessarily always chasing after continental ways and fashions. A very interesting example, which will be looked at in more detail in Chapter Eight, is the statement made by Julius Caesar in his *De Bello Gallico* ('On the Gallic War'), that Britain was the centre of the powerful druidic cult, which was also prevalent among the Gauls. Perhaps archaeologists and historians have been unduly influenced by the modern view of the 'Celtic fringe'. The notion of this region as a repository of ancient custom and practice has been dissected in *The Celts* by

Malcolm Chapman, who reveals it as more like the high-tide-mark zone of relatively recent cultural detritus:

> ' . . . what comes to be seen as timelessly and typically "Celtic", is always the latest "old-fashion" within the more general British context.'

Thus, Scottish country dancing 'continues the dances of polite society throughout Europe 200 years before', though it has acquired a few 'Celtic' tweaks in its last refuge. But there is no reason to suppose that this later state of affairs existed in the centuries immediately preceding the Common Era.

Having said that, we do not know much in detail about social life in Britain and Ireland in the period before the successful Roman invasion of 43CE, which established the imperial province of Britannia. The notion of long-limbed red-haired iron-weapon-wielding aristocratic warriors pushing their way ashore in droves in successive invasions, from about 700BCE, and imposing drastic change, has been rejected. Influences affecting language, culture, and politics did come in from outside, but unevenly, slowly. Even small population movements helped, as when, later, groups of diehard British warriors removed to the north of the Antonine Wall in the second century CE. In such cases, the contribution to social life may have been of a reactionary, rather than a progressive, nature but the pattern of development is never likely to be uniformly in one single direction. The only significant invasion or migration still countenanced is from the immediate post-prehistoric period: the removal of large numbers of the continental Belgae into south Britain, and probably southern Ireland, vouched for by Julius Caesar in *De Bello Gallico* around 54BCE, and which has clear evidence in tribal names and the development of continental-style coinage. This does not imply that in the prehistoric period all the tribes were at a similar level of social organisation or cultural activity at any particular time, or that they were all of the same racial origin, or that there was no movement of population groups at all. The views first noted by Roman commentators have been justified; they wrote that the inhabitants of Britain believed that they had always been there. By these inhabitants they meant the *p*–Celtic speaking tribes who formed the Romano-British population of the province of Britannia and who were closely related to the tribes of southern Scotland.

Current knowledge and its gaps are summed up in the present condition of the great site known as Navan Fort, near Armagh, in Ireland. A hillfort was set up here in the course of the Bronze Age, and in the late stage a round house and circular stockade were built within it. The skull of a Barbary ape has been recovered from here. In the subsequent centuries of the Iron Age, there was often intense building activity. A great and much-disturbed earth bank encircles the whole site, containing within it various other earthworks and the remains of stone structures. The highest point is a tumulus with a single wall. The round house upon it was rebuilt nine times in the period between 700 and 100BCE. This frequency may be related to the durability of the 275 timber poles that supported it: there were five concentric rings of these, with some evidence to show an exceptionally tall post at the centre. The diameter of the whole is 40m (130 ft). A conical thatch or turf roof is assumed to have covered the entire building. At a late stage, around 95BCE, the whole interior was stacked full with limestone blocks and boulders, and the timbers then set alight. It was then covered in a mound of turves. While the physical history of the site can be traced, the reason for such an action as this remains a mystery. The site was not abandoned at that time: it continued in use for another 400 or 500 years, until its final destruction and abandonment in the tribal wars that tore fourth-century Ulster apart. Navan Fort is believed to correspond to the site, famous in Irish legend, of Emain Macha, ancient capital of the Ulaid, the tribal group whose name survives in that of Ulster. As the capital of Conchobar macNessa, it is linked with the great tales of Cuchulainn, some of the central episodes of the 'Heroic Age' of Irish history.

Grand and thought-provoking though they are, the visible remains of Emain Macha seem a pale reflection of the mythic capital that invisibly occupies the same site. Thanks to the legends of the 'Ulster Cycle', the visitor can picture the scene where so many marvels and amazing events occurred, from its founding by the warrior-queen Macha, who forced her five nephews to dig out its first ramparts. One can look out and envisage the fabled race at the end of which the goddess-queen Macha gave birth to twins and cursed the men of Ulster for nine generations, a curse that still had its effect when the Cattle Raid of Cooley took place and Cuchulainn alone had to hold the fort against the army of Connacht, and slew his best friend in doing so. Here rose the 'Red Branch House' that was Conchobar's palace, the ultimate in magnificence and splendour that the Irish Iron Age could create, both in reality and in imagination.

From around 300BCE, life in Britain seems to have been sufficiently free from internecine warfare, and the population sufficiently large, for extensions of agriculture into previously marginal land. Rather than a few fields cleared from a wide space, the landscape was being viewed as an entirety in farming terms, where it was suitable for cultivation, with drainage ditches and hedgerows appearing between the fields, which remained small and rectangular in shape. These 'enclosures' imply a new kind of landownership, maybe on a personal basis rather than a communal one. Settlements became more numerous and were in the open countryside, their lack of defences suggesting that the need for defence was not felt. The type of settlement ranged from single farmsteads to closed-packed village communities, surrounded by fields. Across two great and many lesser islands and hundreds of separate communal groups, there was no consistent state of development.

For reasons of geographical proximity, as well as the presence of immigrant Belgae groups, there were close resemblances

between the societies of the southeast and those in present-day
Belgium and northeast France. Similarly, there were links
between southern and southwestern tribes, and those of
Armorica (Brittany). One of the Armorican tribes, the Veneti,
seem to have controlled the western approaches until their
shattering defeat in a sea battle with the Romans in 56BCE.
The southwestern tribes shared building styles with the
Armoricans, notably the underground storage rooms known in
Cornwall as *fogous*, and a specialised version of the hillfort, the
'cliff castle', utilising the many isolated or semi-isolated coastal
promontories, which afforded ideal defensive sites, though
defence may not have been the prime requirement; like many
hillforts, they may have been exchange and collection centres.
Cliff castles are also a feature of the Irish coast, not always on
promontories – Dun Aengus, on Inishmore in the Aran
Islands, is simply a great fortified semicircle terminating in a
sheer cliff. More typical as living accommodation was the rath,
a circular enclosure with an earth wall, about 30m (120ft) in
diameter, with a circular main building having a central hearth,
and some smaller huts for storage or specialised activities. The
walls might be of wickerwork or timber-and-turf construction.
At least one example has been found (Deer Park Farms, Co.
Antrim), with a double wicker wall packed with insulating
moss and straw.

It should always be remembered that, though stone provides
the durable and visible remains, in most places wood was the
chief building material, along with daub, straw, and leaves. In
Wales, for example, no stone dwelling from before the Iron Age
(around 500BCE) has been identified. A simple palisade of
stakes is likely to have been the protection of most homes. In
central Europe, however, where riches and rivalries were at
a far higher level, protection from one another became more
important. Hillforts, surrounded by massive ramparts, were
established, some of them with whole 'towns' inside for the population to reside, or seek protection, in. Around the middle of

the millennium, the numbers of hillforts increased rapidly. Of the 500+ identified in Wales, many are relatively small, the majority being of less than five hectares in extent, and some 200 being under half a hectare: refuges for an extended family group and their animals rather than true forts. The builders of these forts were principally pastoralists, though they also culti-vated wheat, barley, and flax in small fields, where shelter allowed. Evidence of metalworking has also been found at some fort sites, such as Dinorben in Denbighshire and Breidden in Powys; at these the patronage and protection of a local chief or king allowed the bronze- and tinsmiths to practise their craft in security. Many forts were used only on particular occasions, such as special assemblies for trade or ritual, apart from serving as refuges. Over the centuries, they were often rebuilt, extended, or reduced. Their concentration is greatest in the southwest, though the majority here are small. Often, they are coastal features, and anyone walking the Pembroke coastal path will come across 'cliff castles' of this type. Larger forts are more common on the eastern side, where a sequence follows the line of the Black Mountains and the Berwyns, overlooking the Wye and Severn valleys. Among the largest is Llanymynech, in a district where copper was mined. In the same region, Oswestry Old Fort is one of the best preserved in site and out-line, its rampart walls and ditches still sharp and steep in pro-file. The huts within the forts, ranging in number from one or two to 150 or more, were roundhouses. A thick wall of stones and turf with a single entrance provided a base for a pitched roof of thatch, with a central smoke-hole for the fire. The building of Welsh hillforts effectively came to an end with the Roman occupation.

The oldest iron artefact found in Wales is a sword, from Llyn Fawr, in the mountains above the Rhondda, dating from about 600BCE. At such a time, it would have been among the first, with very few of its kind. This remarkably preserved weapon, probably made in Britain, is of Hallstatt style in such details as the chape, or base-plate, of the scabbard. An iron sickle, made on the model of an older bronze one, was also found, as well as bronze spear- and axe-heads, and two bronze cauldrons. Some writers believe that the Llyn Fawr items were thrown there for hiding, by raiders caught with their booty, but they may have been placed as ritual offerings. For a long time, iron remained a prestige metal, and bronze, stone, and bone also remained very much in use. From this era grew the legend of the smith-god Gofannon, incorporated into old Welsh mythology as a son of the mother-goddess Don, and who, in the *Mabinogi*, sharpens the plough of Amaethon for Culhwch.

Little is known in detail of how the tribes in Wales were organised, though a few hints can be gathered from the archaeological record. The many small forts of the Demetae in the southwest, for instance, suggest a tribal structure based on small groups, perhaps members of an extended family, and without a strong central authority. While small forts are found in the territories of the other tribes, they are dominated by larger ones, suggesting both a larger overall population and more important centres of authority. No site is known definitely to have been that of a tribal overking, though Llanmelin, in the lands of the Silures, is a strong candidate for their principal centre. It was deliberately replaced by the Romans with the cantonal centre of Venta Silurum (later Caerwent).

A very distinctive style of architecture is found in the western and northern islands and the mainland of Scotland, where, from around 200BCE, the brochs were constructed. These buildings, remarkable in their use of unmortared freestone, have been much discussed, particularly the degree to which they were defensive. All commentators are agreed that prestige or display played a part, but the widely spread distribution and the lack of anything that could be called a superbroch suggests that, like the Demetae, the broch-builders were independent communities with no wider regional political structure.

Perhaps they were trying to impress one another, or possibly a different interpretation needs to be sought. One aspect of interest is that no broch has been recorded as having been subject to the vitrification process, whereby creation of brushwood fire outside causes the stonework to partially melt. Such a process would have been fatal to any occupants. Possibly the defensive notion should not be overstressed either.

Among the most frequently found relics of Bronze-Age and Iron-Age life in the British Isles are burned mounds. These are low mounds of charcoal and broken stone, usually now covered in vegetation, which betoken the former existence of a heating trough. The trough itself was a stone-lined pit, sealed with clay, and almost always close to a source of running water. A hearth was set up nearby, in which stones were brought to extreme heat and then placed in the water, heating it to boiling point. Burned mounds were first assumed to have been cooking places where meat could be boiled. The traditional Irish name, *fulacht fiadh*, 'cook-pit of deer', is indicative of this. But, often, there is no evidence in them of animal remains, as might be expected. Another suggested use is as hot baths or sauna-type baths: some Orkney mounds have low walls, suggesting that they might have been roofed over as 'sweat lodges'. Another school of thought has proposed a use in cloth-preparing – either fulling or dyeing – or perhaps as a laundry site. To this might be added the concept of ritual – something that would have accompanied all these procedures, especially among a people whose religion was strongly water-related. All these uses are plausible; perhaps all are true.

In the great hoard of ironware found at Llyn Cerrig Bach, on the druidic island of Anglesey, slave chains were included, dating back to before the Roman period. Either there was an export trade in slaves or a local use of them, probably both. The existence of such a trade; the apparent peace across wide areas of countryside; the enclosures of farming land – these factors, so increasingly evident in the course of the first century BCE, suggest the trend towards a society that was not communities of peasant-farmers but one with an aristocracy. This is borne out by the evidence of high-caste decorated artefacts, particularly mirrors, but also items of personal decoration, beautifully made in a decorative style reminiscent of La Tène. Even if we allow for loss across the centuries, the number of such items is quite small, suggesting that they were the property only of a privileged few. Whether this upper class was native or immigrant, the social pattern certainly seems to be formed on continental models. Nora Chadwick, in *The Celts*, says that:

'On the eve of the conquest the people were still in a heroic age of society.'

Certain customs and practices were localised, or confined to single regions. Southern English tribes, like the Catuvellauni, under Belgic influence, or possibly Belgic themselves, were using coins before the Romans came, while those to the north of them were not. Graves in Kent and other southeastern locations, from the first century BCE, held pots and other food or wine containers from as far away as Italy. Pottery-making had become more of a specialist process, using the wheel, and wheel-made pottery was used much more than the handmade pots of earlier centuries. The Belgae had brought a way and a view of life already partly adjusted to the colonial Roman mode.

CHAPTER SIX

The Empire Strikes

After Caesar's expeditions, almost 90 years went by, with the British Isles still beyond the limit of empire, but linked with it by a pattern of trading and diplomatic contacts. Some British tribal leaders made alliances with the Romans, while others remained aloof. In 43AD, in the reign of the emperor Claudius, the Romans made the decisive move to reduce Britannia to an imperial province. Four legions were landed, at Richborough in Kent, and met little resistance as they pushed northwards to capture *Camulodunum* (Colchester), centre of a strong Belgic kingdom that had until a short time before been ruled by Cunobelinus. The emperor himself made a brief visit to this remote and exotic new addition to the Roman world. His general, Aulus Plautius, extended Roman rule over the southeast regions, from the Wash to Southampton Water. But the further the invaders went from the southeast, the more fierce and hostile were the native inhabitants. In the southwest, and west of the Severn, and north of Trent, only hard fighting and military occupation secured the Roman position. In 61 a rebellion broke out in a region they had thought pacified, when the East Anglian Iceni tribe rose, under its queen Boudicca, and attacked and destroyed the Roman camp-towns of *Camulodunum*, *Verulamium* (St Albans) and *Londinium* (London) with great ferocity. Boudicca, who had no son, had claimed to rule after the death of her husband; presumably in accordance with custom. But the Romans refused this and whipped her and her daughters.

> 'In a chariot, with her daughters in front of her, Boudica went to tribe after tribe, arguing that it was in truth proper for the Britons to fight under the leadership of a woman. "But now," she said, "it is not as a woman of aristocratic descent, but as one of the people, that I take vengeance for lost freedom, for my lashed body, for the violated virginity of my daughters . . . If you consider fully the power of the hosts and the grounds for the war, you will see that in this battle you must prevail or die. This is a woman's determination. As for the men, they may live and be slaves." '
>
> Tacitus, *Annals*

Tacitus seems to be suggesting that it was not a natural thing for a woman to assume rule, but he may have been putting matters in terms that made more sense to a Roman reader. The governor, Suetonius Paulinus, who had been campaigning in northwest Wales against the tribe of Ordovices, hastily returned and defeated the Iceni, and heavy and drastic reprisals followed. Boudicca poisoned herself. The British tribes had certainly not lived in a state of mutual peace, but the organised terror of Roman colonial warfare was a new and horrifying experience for them. If the Roman army brought civilisation in its wake, it first prepared the ground by burning, rape, plunder, extortion and mass killings.

It was with a campaign of virtual genocide that the governor Agricola, appointed to Britain in 78 and in charge until 85, smashed the Ordovices and established control of the great tribe of the Brigantes, whose territory lay right across the country north of the Humber. Three great legionary fortresses were set up to sustain Roman rule, at *Eboracum* (York), *Deva* (Chester) and *Isca* (Caerleon); each placed to give quick access to the still doubtful hill districts. For three hundred years the country would be Romano-British, though most of the garrison soldiers were not Roman or even Italian, but from eastern Europe: present-day Romania and the Adriatic coastal states. Many of them settled after long service, and veterans' colonies were set up at Lincoln, Colchester and Gloucester. Roman life and influence was strongest in the towns, and the countryside retained its Brittonic speech and Celtic lifestyle. The Romans had however eradicated, or tried very hard to eradicate, their druidical religion, whose great centre had been the island of Anglesey. The druids, priests, counsellors, prophets and lore-masters, had been seen as the prime source of anti-Roman agitation, and a torrent of propaganda was turned on them, as well as military force. Though worship of the Celtic gods and nature spirits certainly continued, and the Romans were not hostile to the local gods, the campaign against the druids and their cult may have helped to create a religious vacuum from which Christianity would later benefit.

The events in Britannia were watched with keen interest from west and north. When the emperor Claudius came to Colchester, a deputation from Orkney came to offer submission in return for protection – clearly all was not harmony in the far north. When Agricola reached the Galloway shore, he was met by an Irish chieftain who encouraged the Roman general to invade and offered to be his ally: shades of king Dermot McMurrough a thousand years on. The Romans, however, had enough to do in attempting the conquest of the Caledonians. The tribes of Hibernia were never invaded and remained free to fight one another and maintain the same kind of life they had been living for centuries. But isolation should not be taken to mean they did not continue to keep a close eye on events in the Roman province and elsewhere. For one thing, the Romans now controlled their export-import trade. A trading station was set up on Irish soil. But wherever on the coast of Gaul or Britain an Irish vessel beached for trading, a Roman or Romanised official would not be not far away, to keep a record and levy the tax due on imports into the empire.

From the arrival of the Romans in northern Gaul, the names of tribes begin to be recorded.

It may be partly from Roman army maps and reports that the list of tribes and places made by the Greek geographer Claudius Ptolemy, at Alexandria, around 150, for inclusion in his world atlas, was compiled, though some of Ptolemy's information was older – perhaps as old as Pytheas – and possibly already out of date. He names some 24 tribes in Britain and another 14 or so in Ireland. Some can only be identified from a geographical name; thus Ptolemy's 'cape of the Novantae' (now the Mull of Galloway) identifies both the tribe and its location in southwest Scotland. Much reliance has been put on Ptolemy's list of tribes, though it does not include the Boresti of northern Scotland, noted by Tacitus, nor the Maeatae and Attacotti who are mentioned in later writings. It gives tribal names on the two mainlands only, though most of the larger islands are listed, as well as the Ebudae, later miswritten as Hebrides. In two cases, tribal names recur in different areas: Brigantes in northern England and southeast Ireland; and Cornavii in north Scotland and southwest England. Perhaps the Dumnonii in southwest England, and the Damnonii in southern Scotland, should be added. Though some scholars have supposed a Brigantian colony of Brittonic speakers established among the Gaels – perhaps not the only one; the French Celticist Henri Hubert also believed that the Irish Brigantians' neighbouring Manapi tribe were a Belgic colony – there may be other reasons for the parallel names. Hubert also sees the name of the Gangani in the names Gann and Genann, leaders of the Fir Bolg, who landed at the mouth of the Shannon (see Chapter Ten). Some tribal names may be totemic, relating to an animal spirit, as with the Epidii, 'horse people'; their home on the Mull of Kintyre is Ptolemy's Epidion Akron, 'horse promontory'. Some may be purely topographical: Cornavii is believed to include the meaning 'horn' and both tribes of that name live in peninsular areas which could be described as 'horns'. There is very little correspondence between

Ptolemy's tribal names and later place names. In Wales, Degannwy is linked to the tribe of the Decantae. On the Ross-Sutherland border, in Scotland, the hill of Carn Sméart has been linked with the Smertae tribe, whose name seems to mean 'smeared ones'; and in Argyll, very tentatively, Crinan with the Creones. The clearest links are with the Caledones, found in three Perthshire names: Dunkeld and Rohallion, both meaning 'fort of the Caledonians', and the mountain Schiehallion, 'fairy hill of the Caledonians'. Ptolemy also names numerous locations, mostly rivers and headlands, with a few town-sites. Two of his Irish sites are simply noted as 'royal capital'; one equates closely with Emain Macha in Ulster, the other has been more tentatively linked with Cruachan, an important prehistoric site in Connacht, associated with the legendary queen Medbh. Ptolemy's work, available not from his original but only from Renaissance re-creations, raises as many questions as it answers, but it remains the most complete list of the Insular Celtic tribes around and before 150AD.

Tacitus in 'Agricola' (90AD) refers to the country as Caledonia and the inhabitants as Britanni, lumping them in with all the native inhabitants of Britain, but he also refers to their *civitates*, or states, and names different tribal groups. He also considered them to be of different physical appearance to the other Britanni, large and long-limbed, 'like the Germans', he thought. Ptolemy in 150 refers to the Caledones in a manner which implies they are one of a number of tribes. Around 200, the Roman writer Cassius Dio, whose work survives only in a condensed copy from medieval times, mentions the Maiatai, living next to the Wall (assumed to be Antonine's) and the Kaledonioi who live beyond them. In 297, comes the panegyrist Eumenius's mention of Picti, followed in 310 by that of *Calidonum aliorumque Pictorum*, 'Caledonians and other Picts'. Ammianus Marcellinus, describing events in 368, says *Picti in duas gentes divisi, Dicalydonas et Verturiones*, 'the Picts are divided into two groups, Dicaledonians and Verturiones'. Marjorie

Anderson makes the point that he may be only referring to specific raiding groups and not the whole people of the Picts. In 398 the panegyrist Claudian writes that 'Thyle [the sea] waxed hot with blood of Picts', referring to Stilicho's campaign against them. Around 490, a Latin life of St Germanus refers to the 'Alleluia battle' he fought against the Picts, and around the same time St Patrick wrote his complaint about the 'evil and apostate Picts' who were taking Christians as slaves.

These tribes – the peoples west of the Irish Sea and north of Hadrian's Wall – existed on a very different basis to that which the Romans set up in their province to the south. The Romans and Romano-Britons were town-dwellers whose economic life was based on the use of money in exchange for goods and services, part of a firmly imposed fiscal system which applied the proceeds of taxation to the maintenance of a large standing army, a large bureaucracy, and the manifold activities of the Imperial Household (whose functions merged into that of the bureacracy). In many ways, though distorted by injections of plunder from conquest, and by slavery, it was a market-based economy. Large farms, with Roman-style villas as their headquarters, supplied produce both for urban markets and for provision to the army. The independent tribes, though they also acquired plunder and kept slaves, had no such structure. They were country dwellers whose economic system had no need for money. The wealth of the tribe and of its leaders was measured in agricultural terms, chiefly in cows; the prestige of its leaders was measured in fighting men and in their own capacity for display and generous gift-giving. Settlements needed to be self-sufficient in basic foods: cereals, chiefly barley, and beans and early forms of brassicas were grown. Animals were kept for milk, draught and meat. The extent of the farm-land, and its defensibility, effectively limited the growth potential of the community. Arable farming, pastoral farming – including the practice of transhumance, with the annual removal of the animals and their male and female attendants to upland pastures – and trapping, fishing and hunting, all with many supporting activities, were practised and must have taken up most of the community's time and energy, even allowing for slave labour.

Among the Irish and the Britons (and probably the Picts), the social organisation was that of a kindred group, in which each person had a defined role and made a specific contribution. In return, each received a share of the tribe's produce and participated in its social activities and ceremonies. Some early 20th-century writers felt that this was a primitive form of communism, but there was nothing democratic about it; the tribal community was rigidly divided into social groups, whose status was fixed. Heredity – the fortune of being born into the right family – wealth, and the skill to manage and increase that wealth, determined success. Fields and cows were owned by those who were of sufficient status, and were worked on behalf of the owner by those of lower rank, and by slaves. The contributions of slave labour to the workforce, and of the sale of slaves to the rulers' wealth, are impossible to assess, but they may have been substantial. The upper ranks comprised warriors, who were required to own weapons (and, until the first century BC, chariots and horses), and the 'professional' groups who in addition to bards and druids embraced the skills of lawmen, doctors, smiths, fine metal-workers, carpenters, shipwrights and, in later centuries, stone-carvers and scribes.

In these communities, wealth flowed upwards. The splendour of the king or chief was the glory of his people or tribe. His riches were used for conspicuous display, seen at its most apparent in the tribute given to the gods, in the decoration of his house and the magnificence of his feasts; and in the opulence of his gifts. In addition to the produce of his own herds, flocks, fields and fisheries, he was due a share of everyone else's. Although the claims on his own hospitality were very great, he was also entitled to claim the hospitality of his subchiefs: these ancient forms of taxation in kind, respectively known as 'kain' and 'conveth', lived on into medieval Scotland. A famous Old Irish poem, 'The

Vision of MacConglinne', recounts in comic form the depredations a greedy king could make on his chieftains, reducing them to penury. In the 18th century, a Scottish cottar's wife was still required to provide 'kain' eggs and butter to the laird, and complaints about 'kain' and 'conveth' were made as late as the Napier Commission on Crofting in 1884. The importance laid by the rulers on maintaining their due share was always great. Of the battle of Monith Carno in 729, between the rival Pictish kings Oengus and Nechtan, it is specially noted that among those killed were the *exactatores*, 'tribute collectors' of Nechtan.

Underpinning this system, apart from the force of tradition, was the fact that it was in its essentials common to a set of neighbouring peoples. Its resilience and strength were shown by the fact that it survived alongside the very different economy and government of Roman Britain for more than three centuries, and lived on long after the Romans had gone. The later-coming Anglians and Vikings (though the latter were more commercially-minded) maintained social and economic systems that were broadly compatible. In the last resort, however, it was territory that mattered. The occupation and tenure of its land was the real guarantee of security to a tribe or a people. In the legends shared by Scots and Irish, the encounter of the Milesians with the triad of Ériu, Banba and Fótla, goddesses of the land and soil, is a very significant one, confirming a potent bond between land and people; and we shall see that there are signs in place names of that bond having been imported to the landscape of Scotland.

In international trade, the territories of Ireland and Scotland had relatively little to offer. There were no tin deposits, and the gold seems to have been largely exhausted. The Romans exploited the lead mines at Wanlockhead, in the Scottish southern uplands, where there was also silver to be found, but while they may have enriched the Selgovae chiefs, and later the kings of Strathclyde, ores from here do not seem to have been exported. North Wales had richer lead deposits. Bog ore deposits may have provided a limited amount of low-quality iron for local

smelting. This developing contact has been traced in the archaeological record at Dunadd in Argyll, and a number of key hillforts in Ireland, including Clogher, County Tyrone, and Tara,
were the main centres of such trade as there was. They were used
as collection and distribution points. The outward traffic was
probably chiefly in furs, especially white winter pelts, and in
hides and feathers, pearls and semiprecious stones. Evidence of
inward traffic can still be found in remains of pottery jugs and
jars, beads and glassware. The rath at Garranes in County Cork
has been identified as a likely storage-site for imported pottery in
the fifth and sixth centuries, and there may well be others. It has
been suggested that wine was imported in barrels, which will not
have survived; and other items, such as quality cloth garments,
would also have perished. Imported goods then were trans-
ported inland, presumably in exchange for local products. The
least amount of evidence for imports has been found in Pictland.
No import-distribution centre to be compared with Dunadd
seems to have existed on the east coast. But even in remote parts
of Pictland, remains of imported objects have been found on
domestic sites, from Roman glassware to jet ornaments.

Sometime between 222 and 235CE, a carved stone tablet was
put up in a temple of the Imperial cult at Camulodunum
(Colchester in southeast England). This place was both a major
centre of the British Iceni tribe and a Roman garrison town. The
Latin inscription tells that Lossio Ueda, a Caledonian, *nepos*
(nephew or possibly grandson) of Uepogenus, made a dedication to the god-emperor. Professor Kenneth Jackson has demon-
strated both names to be Pictish, and linked the latter name to
Uipoig namet, one of the earlier entries in the Pictish king-list (see
Chapter Ten). Apart from the tablet's linguistic significance, it is
of interest in showing contact between Picts and Romans at a
time not long after the Severan invasions of 208–11. Lossio Ueda
was clearly a person of high status. Although he could have paid
for the inscription to be carved without himself knowing Latin, it
is more probable that he had some knowledge of that language,

in order to be able to talk to Romans. The purpose of his visit is not known, though placing the tablet suggests an official mission of some kind; and the little episode, accidentally-discovered, is another reminder of how much we do not know about events and diplomatic relations at this time.

The chief resources of Ireland and Pictland were stone, wood, water, and space – enough of all these to allow for the establishment of viable settlements, but nothing to draw the interest of far-off capitalists, or to foster a vibrant economic life. At least until they were able to obtain blackmail payments from the Romans in return for peace; and later to plunder the rich villas of Roman Britain, the kings of the Caledonians were relatively poor. Such efforts as they could make towards the models of opulent display as found in the 'élite' burial sites of the British tribes of eastern England, for example, would be modest, and help to explain the lack of such finds in Ireland and Pictland (though factors such as the dampness and acidity of the soil also may have contributed to the decay of artefacts).

Evidence of the nature of 'Dark Age' social life is hard to come by. Some of the buildings that have been traced were big enough to hold quite large gatherings, but no building has been identified as having the function of a hall, or assembly room, and nothing else. From the early literature of the Irish we know of feasts in wood-built halls where the king, his leading men, his bards and his warriors gathered and where the champion's portion was hotly disputed; and the archaeological finds of bronze and iron cauldrons (and what may be cauldron-symbols on later Pictish carved stones) indicate that cooking vessels of substantial size were available. How far social life was communal and how much it was based more on the single family, is not known. The presence of a large number of grinding querns on the site of the Dunadd fortress suggests that this wearisome aspect of food-production was communal – or industrial: the work may have been done by slave-labour. Some writers, taking their evidence from various fragments available, have made wide claims about family life, like W. H. Murray in his *Islands of Western Scotland*: 'Among the Picts and early Scots there was no family life in the narrow sense, for the sanction of marriage was unknown. Men and women had a free sexual relationship, and the children of each community were reared as joint offspring.' This vision of free love and *kibbutz*-style nurseries in the pre-Christian Hebrides is a sweeping assumption rather than a provable statement. (It is notable, though, that right up to modern times, marriage and divorce in Scotland were more informal procedures than in most western European countries.)

In Wales, there was a lesser degree of integration with a Roman way of life than among the Romano-Britons to the east, with the exception of the relatively small towns at Caerleon and Carmarthen. While the country was pacified and demilitarised, the tribes seem to have retained their own habitations and way of life, though not without Roman influence. In the south they were displaced by Roman owners from most of the best farming land. Close to their centre at Caerleon, Roman-type villas were established: more like large country farm-estates than anything else. As well as the land-owner's house, built round its courtyard in standard Roman fashion, it had outhouses, sheds and barns to accommodate the work, the workers and their produce. The famous villa excavated at Llantwit Major, with its own bath-house, is the best-known example. Estates almost as large were founded in the vicinity of the fort and Roman town at Carmarthen. The Romans were keen exploiters of whatever the land could offer, so long as it was worth a merchant's investment, and they were mining gold at Dolaucothi, near Carmarthen, on an industrial scale, using water power, and employing both open-cast and tunnelling techniques. Such enterprises were under strict imperial control, though contractors might have been employed to do the work. Lead and silver were also extracted in the north, around Flint, where coal was also mined for the smelting furnaces; and copper continued to be mined in Anglesey. Slaves are likely to have been the basic work force in these enterprises and on the country estates. Although the great bulk of mineral product was removed further afield, native metalworking still persisted outside areas of Roman influence, and brooches and ornamental metal wares decorated in local versions of the La Tène style continued to be made.

Although the Romans sought to stamp out the cult of the druids, or some aspects of it, this was more because of the powerful part played by the cult in nourishing a sense of independence, than because of any specifically religious practice. So long as religion remained within certain bounds, and did not offend the Romans' not very highly developed sense of propriety, they were quite happy for a whole variety of cults to flourish. Their chief requirement – certainly for anyone aspiring to Roman citizenship – was that the 'imperial cult' should also be honoured. Its was the chief temple in any Roman town, and civic dignitaries like the *decuriones* of Caerwent were compelled to support and officiate in the cult of the deified emperor and his ancestors, at least if these were also of imperial blood. Consequently, pagan Celtic and pagan Roman worship went on side by side, and each often borrowed or blended aspects of the other. The Romans had a tendency everywhere to assimilate local deities to their own pantheon. Julius Caesar claimed firmly that the Celts worshipped Mercury, Apollo, Mars, Jupiter and Minerva, when in fact he meant that they worshipped gods whose aspects corresponded to some aspects at least of those classical deities. The religion of the tribes resembled that of the Romans in that it was one of ritual observance rather than intense personal dedication. This does not imply insincerity or indifference; merely that the gods were an impersonal force who did not demand impassioned and exclusive commitment. This enabled both forms of paganism to co-exist and intermingle.

As a result of the Roman occupation, the ancestral form of modern Welsh took in many Latin loan words, most of which have come through into modern Welsh. Such words show what the Romans had that the Welsh tribes did not; and the areas in which the two sides came into contact. Military engineering terms like *ffos*, trench, *pont*, bridge, *castell*, castle, form one area. Writing is another, with *llyfr, book, llythyr*, letter, and *ysgrif*, script, among others. The Romans' superiority in architecture and building is shown by the borrowing of such words as *ffenestr*, window, *ystafell*, chamber, and *colofn*, pillar. Many domestic items, such as *cyllell*, knife, *ffiol*, bowl, *cannwl*, candle, come from Latin. *Cadair*, throne, is another borrowing, but, unlike the Gaels, the Welsh did not use the Latin *rex* for king, retaining instead the traditional *brenin*. As Sir John Lloyd pointed out in his history of Wales, although popular speech may employ words like *pobl*, people, and *estron*, foreigner, the language of Welsh law, harking back to an older tradition, has very few Latin terms other than *tyst*, witness. Latin also gave the Welsh a number of first names, at least one of which remains current today, Emrys, from *Ambrosius*.

The nature of relationships between the sexes, and the status of women among the insular peoples, is open to debate. The Irish story of the *Táin Bó Cuailgne* makes Medbh at least the equal of her husband Ailill. A long tradition of female warriors existed in Ireland and in Scotland. The law-books of the Irish *brehons* (see Chapter Eleven) indicate that in many ways women had a legal status equivalent to that of men. Among the Britons the status of women appears to have been lower: in *When Was Wales?*, Gwyn A. Williams notes the ambiguity of a system in which women in one sense were scarcely more than chattels.

'They were considered weak and inferior, in need of a protector . . . Yet Welsh women came to be identified as the gift-givers and while they were not apparently as free as their Irish cousins, they seem to have been more free and independent than many ordinary women of the Europe of their time.'

There were circumstances in which a woman could be a reigning queen, as with Boudicca and her contemporary Cartimandua, queen of the Brigantes, who appears to have been of higher rank than her husband Venutius (whom she discarded in favour of his armour-bearer).

As an aside, it may be noted that three classical writers referred to the practice of homosexuality among the continental Celts. One is Aristotle (fourth century BCE) who makes a passing reference in his *Politics* to 'the Celts and certain other groups who openly approve of sexual relations between men'. Three hundred years later, just before the Christian era, Diodorus Siculus wrote:

> 'The men of the Gauls pay little attention to their women, even though they are quite beautiful, but prefer unnatural intercourse with other men. They sleep on the ground on the skins of wild animals, rolling about with their sleeping companions on each side . . . they gladly offer their youthful bodies to others, not thinking this any disgrace, but being deeply offended when refused.'

Writing a generation or two later, the geographer Strabo makes a similar assertion, though both he and Diodorus Siculus rely on hearsay and show a degree of anti-Celtic prejudice. If such extreme forms of male bonding were common in any of the kingdoms of the British Isles, they are not recorded, even by those who might have seized on such practices as evidence of depravity.

Celtic society has often been characterised as 'war-mad', from the first-century geographer Strabo onwards; a description which is increasingly being challenged. From Caesar on, most of the descriptions in the historical period have been made by those who were at war with the Celtic tribes, or who saw them as potential enemies. It is not surprising that they portrayed them with a warlike aspect. But it was the Romans who invaded the Britons and Caledonians. The scanty historical records of the Scots and Picts, with their frequent mentions of battles, have also tended to overstress the role of warfare. Fortifications survive in the landscape, and metal weapons are preserved more readily than wooden ploughshares or horn tools. Then as now, storytellers and their hearers relished the drama of warfare, and the opportunities for heroism it provided. None of this need imply an obsession with war. The regular preoccupations of the tribes are more likely to have been with the land and its cultivation; and with the rites and festivals to accompany it, than with warfare. The notion of war-madness has been encouraged by the recognition of the warrior-class in these societies: the aristocratic group, supported by freemen farmers and slaves, whose role was to provide the fighting force of the tribe and the kingdom. But it might be as accurate to call them the hunting class. The carved art of Pictland shows as much of hunts as it does of battles. These people had the leisure, the equipment, the wealth and the social status to engage in events that promoted personal display and individual prowess. And there is no reason to suppose that these displays were not appreciated and relished by those whose status debarred them from participation.

'If you wish for peace, prepare for war' is an old Roman maxim, taken to heart by many other peoples, especially after they got to know something of the Romans. Apart from self-defence against invasion from outside, as by Romans, Angles and Norsemen, the wars fought by the inhabitants of England, Wales, Ireland and Scotland since the Roman period have two main causes. The first is in the protection of territory, and the second is strife over the kingship. From what we know of the institutions of law, little as it is, it is fair to assume that in both cases armed struggle was normally a last resort after the failure of law or diplomacy to resolve matters. From the sixth century on, the records of the Synods of Drum Ceatt and of Birr, and there were others, make it clear that at these church-sponsored gatherings, intercommunal affairs were discussed and efforts made to resolve disputes.

Chapter Seven

The Expansion of the Gaels

The third century and the first decades of the fourth were a time of relative stability and prosperity within the Roman colony. Military activity was focused on continuing attempts to suppress the warrior peoples of Caledonia. Roman troops could gain fighting experience in the badlands north of Hadrian's Wall, and massive expeditions were launched from the legionary headquarters at York under the emperor Septimius Severus in 208–09 and the emperor Constantius in 306. Between these imperial visitations, the provincial government was pulled to and fro by the rivalries of would-be military rulers of northwest Europe. From 260, it had been divided into two provinces: Britannia Superior, with its military centres at Chester and Caerleon to the south, and Britannia Inferior, with its headquarters at York, forming the northern province. Britannia was wealthy, its internal stability secured by its three legionary centres, its prosperity sustained by the new urban culture developed under Roman rule, and its – and the army's – purchasing requirements. The towns of Roman Britain were mostly very small, but they were true urban nuclei, trading centres, homes of craftsmen, shopkeepers, and merchants, with public facilities like bathhouses, and with their own local government. A legal distinction was, at first, applied between native peoples and Roman citizens, but this came to an end in 212, in the reign of the emperor Caracalla, when all free-born inhabitants of the empire were granted the rights and status of Roman citizens. The inhabitants of the colony were thus truly Romano-Britons. In Britannia, as elsewhere, this still left a substantial population of slaves, who were the property of their masters and had no civic rights.

In the south, towns grew as open places, at fords or road junctions, or close to an old tribal centre, as with Dorchester and the adjacent hillfort of Maiden Castle. Some were manufacturing places, like the pottery centre of *Durobrivae* (Water Newton) on the River Nene. As a port and commercial centre, London was probably already the largest town, and a centre of civilian administration. The town councils were manned by decurions, citizens whose wealth and status qualified them – often reluctantly – for leadership. Tax collection, and the making-up of any arrears in the assessment, were prime aspects of their responsibility. Latin was the language of these urban communities, though everyone, save transient Roman administrators, must also have spoken Brittonic. The non-British proportion of the population can only be vaguely estimated, but it is unlikely to have exceeded ten per cent of the total at any time. and to have diminished in the fourth and fifth centuries with the reduction in strength of the legionary garrison.

In the first century, the readiness of the Votadini tribe to ally itself with the Romans suggests that it was under pressure from the west, just as the various overtures to the Romans from far-off Orkney suggest that its neighbours to the south of the Pentland Firth were threatening to encroach (this is strongly suggestive of different peoples on each side, but real supporting evidence is lacking).

The figure or description of the naked Celtic warrior, equipped with nothing but sword, shield, and a torc (presumably invested with the qualities of a charm or amulet) round his neck, frequently found in classical sculpture and writings, endured for several centuries. The torc lasted into the sixth century, at least; in the 'Gododdin' poem, we find 'Before

Catraeth there were swift gold-torqued men', though they also wore armour.

The Romans also record that the Gauls and the Picts painted or tattooed their bodies. We have no record of how or for what purpose this was done. In societies that use tattooing and ritual marks, these can indicate some or all of such aspects as rank, status, role, family group, age and maturity, and achievement, as well as talismanic values for protection, or enhancement of skills. All of these could have figured in Pictish body art – the one sure thing is that it would not have been just for 'decoration'. A Roman sculpture from Bridgeness, on the Antonine Wall, shows a Roman cavalryman spearing naked figures whose rectangular shields bear circular motifs. Fighting in the nude appears to have gone out of fashion after the early centuries of the millennium. By the time Pictish figure sculpture appears, the warriors are helmeted, and clad in stout-looking tunics of leather or cloth. The shields are often small and round, as if preserving the centres of the earlier ones. They are armed with swords and spears, sometimes with crossbows (though these are more often seen in hunting scenes than in battles). Evidence of slingshots has also been found in Pictish and British archaeological sites.

The chariots described by Tacitus in the first century had been abandoned, probably by the third century, but horses remained in use, and eighth-century Pictish warriors are shown on horseback bearing spears or lances. They have no stirrups, which must have reduced their effectiveness in hand-to-hand combat. In a stone found above a triple grave at Brough of Birsay, in Orkney, three spear-bearers are shown in what appear to be processional robes, the leader clearly in a more elaborate costume, and they bear ornamented square shields. Cloaked, robed, or tunic-wearing, none of the Pictish figures is clearly seen wearing the *bracae*, or breeches, known to have been worn by the continental Celts.

War-mad the inhabitants may not have been, but they had no aversion to warfare and the hill tribes of west and north did not knuckle under to Roman rule. With one thirtieth of the land of the empire, Britain required the presence of one tenth of the Roman army. The three legionary centres were all close to the edge of upland country – York, Chester, and Caerleon. Such a force at his command made the governor a powerful figure. Between 192 and 196, the governor of Britannia, Clodius Albinus, was distracted from his task by his ambition to become emperor. Backed by his own three legions, he was accepted as a co-ruler by Septimius Severus, who had established himself as emperor at Rome with the support of 16 legions. But it soon became clear that Severus intended to be sole ruler. The northern tribes must have followed rumours and reports of this imperial power game with keen interest. Late in 196, Albinus crossed to Gaul with an army; in February 197, he was defeated and killed by Severus. It seems that, whichever Wall was currently the frontier, it was still manned, as Britannia was not attacked. The Maeatae were unlikely to miss an opportunity to break through, if it had been available.

But, beyond the Wall, the new Roman policy of gifts to ensure peace had the disadvantage that the recipients of the gifts soon wanted more. Cassius Dio reported in 197 that the Caledonians had 'broken their undertakings'. We do not know what these undertakings were or what shifts of policy or power led to their being broken, but the consequences were bloody. Severus sent a new governor to Britannia, Virius Lupus, to restore Roman rule and order; Lupus had to contend with revolt in Wales and among the Brigantes, quite apart from the threatening behaviour of the Maeatae outside the province. The Maeatae were content to be bought off by bribes or subsidies, thereby restoring a buffer between Hadrian's Wall and the Caledones, and giving Lupus and his successors time to batter the Brigantes and the Welsh tribes back into submission. It was 206–07 before the Romans were able to start to restore Hadrian's Wall.

In Volume 1 of *The Decline and Fall of the Roman Empire*, Edward Gibbon indulges in a fascinating aside when discussing Caracalla's war:

> '. . . it is supposed, not without a degree of probability, that the invasion of Severus is connected with the most shining period of the British history or fable. Fingal, whose fame, with that of his heroes and bards, has been revived in our language by a recent publication, is said to have commanded the Caledonians in that memorable juncture, to have eluded the power of Severus, and to have obtained a signal victory on the banks of the Carun, in which the son of *the King of the World*, Caracalla fled from his arms along the fields of his pride.'

Unfortunately for Gibbon, the 'recent publication' mentioned by him is the highly unhistorical 'Ossian' heroic poem confected by James Macpherson and published in 1760, and the degree of probability was, in fact, zero. Fingal, or Finn, was a legendary hero of the Gaels, who at this time were playing a minimal part, if any, in events on Scottish ground. Who commanded the Caledonians against Caracalla is not known. What might be thought strange is that episodes such as the Severan invasion find no echo in authentic later tales and legends. It is however around this time that the 'Heroic Age' of the Gaels was being played out in Ireland. From this era a great body of almost-historical, mythical, and legendary characters and events have been preserved in Europe's oldest literary tradition. 'Ossian' itself and the further 'discoveries' made by Macpherson, in fact cobbled from old manuscripts and the oral tradition and embroidered by Macpherson in a style that is wholly 18th-century, gave a massive boost to the notion of a 'Celtic' Scotland and were immensely popular for half a century.

At the time of Septimius Severus's invasion of Caledonia, Ireland was inhabited by a large number of separate tribes. Each tribe, or *tuath*, was a unit under its own king, although they shared a common culture and language. Their speech was an early form of Gaelic. Among the Irish tribes, the pattern of loyalties and identities was in constant flux. The leaders of stronger tribes or groups of tribes sought to extend their control over others, and this led to frequent warfare among the warrior caste. The concept of an 'overking' with powers over several large groups forming a province, such as Ulster, had been established. But the later notion of an overall 'high king' did not then exist. Even the province was by no means a fixed or centralised kingdom. The overking's role was to arbitrate, to implement generally accepted laws, and to play an important part in priestly rites. Around 21CE, an overking was the famous and semilegendary Conn Cétchathach, 'of the Hundred Battles' or 'Hundred-Fighter', whose stronghold was in Meath, the central part of the island. His by-name was won by fighting the Dál Araidhe people of eastern Ulster, who are recorded as being Cruithne or Picts. He is closely associated with the *Lia Fáil*, the stone of destiny or prophecy, and foretold the future of his own dynasty while seated on it. The expansionist aims of Conn and his successors put severe pressure on the concentration of little kingdoms in Ulster, the northern province of Ireland.

From the third century, refugees from tribal wars crossed the sea eastwards to settle in the underpopulated territory, whose extremities were only 19 kilometres (12 miles) away and easily visible from the land of the Dàl Riata people on the Ulster coast. Forming little Gaelic-speaking enclaves, and living – their chiefs at least – in the same sort of raths or duns they had known in Ireland, and probably still preoccupied by events in Ireland, they made little difference to the state of affairs in Caledonia. Bede, in his *History of the English Church and People*, refers to the first colonisation as taking place under a leader named Reuda, and there is an Irish tradition that Cairpre Riata led a migration to Argyll (or perhaps to Galloway) as early as the third century. It is plain that the inhabitants of northern Britain and Ireland were well aware of one another, and that colonisation from Ireland was taking place on a limited scale well before the traditional founding of Dàl Riada by Fergus MacErc and his sons around 500. It would be likely that diplomatic gift-exchanging and intermarrying took place among ruling families on both sides of the North Channel, though there is no direct evidence from this time. Indications of links are found in some of the tales of the 'Ulster Cycle', centred on the site of Emain Macha, Navan Fort, in Ireland. Their greatest hero, Cuchulainn, was said to have learned the arts of war from a witch-warrior, Scáthach, who lived on Skye; and it was on another of these Amazons from the land of Alba, Aife (who may have been Scáthach by another name), that he first fathered a child. His own birth-name, Sétanta, suggests a British origin, from the tribe of the Setantii.

Further comings and goings between Scotland and Ireland are told in the celebrated account of 'Deirdre of the Sorrows', who escapes with her lover Nóise to an idyllic life in the neighbourhood of Loch Etive, until tragic destiny draws them back to Ireland, treachery, and death. The tales of Fionn mac Cumhaill and his band of poet-warriors would be brought over with the colonists, and remain so popular that their exploits would gradually be identified with the mountains and glens of the new home. 'Have you tales of the Fianna?' was a question that would be hopefully asked of every visitor to a Gaelic-speaking household, into the 19th century.

Roman rule over what later became England and Wales lasted for 400 years and, while its effect on the Britons inhabiting the imperial provinces is obviously most significant, its effect on the independent tribes of Hibernia and Caledonia must have been very considerable (some consequences of this are looked at later in this book). The rulers of the tribes kept themselves well informed of developments in the Roman provinces, and responded with alacrity to any signs of reduced military presence. With the weakening of the western empire, the forays of war bands became an increasingly regular happening. They were particularly successful in 367, a year of disaster for the Roman administration. The events were described by the Roman historian, Ammianus Marcellinus, as a 'barbarian conspiracy': a concerted pattern of assault by the Picts (described as being formed of Dicalydonae and Verturiones – it has been pointed out that this may mean two of a larger number of Pictish tribes, not that they were divided into two only), the Scots, and the Attacotti all invading Britannia, while Franks and Saxons simultaneously attacked Gaul. These were not colonial expeditions but raids, looking for booty and perhaps also for blackmail, and affording opportunities to warriors in the 'heroic culture' to distinguish themselves and acquire prestige and wealth. It was in response to the raids of 367, which may have involved serious battles, since two very senior Roman generals were recorded as missing or killed, that Theodosius was sent to restore order to the beleaguered provinces.

The most famous Gaelic colonist belongs to a somewhat later period. Fergus, son of Erc, has always been a figure of importance to those interested in the pedigree of the Scottish kings. In the past, as the first king of the Dàl Riata of Argyll, he has been regarded as virtually the founder of the Scottish nation. He is first described in the tenth-century document known as the *Senchus fer nAlban*, though its origin is in a document of three centuries earlier. The 'Annals of Tigernach' and those of Clonmacnoise note him, though the 'Annals of Ulster' do not. H. M. Chadwick notes cautiously that the invasion or colonisation 'is traditionally stated to have been led by three princes, Fergus mac Eirc and his two brothers'. Marjorie Anderson says:

'The traditions about the earliest Dàl Riatan settlement of Britain do not inspire great confidence . . . The genealogy seems to reach solid ground with the generation of Comgall and Gabrán, grandsons of Fergus son of Erc.'

In his examination of the *Senchus*, in *Studies in the History of Dalriada*, John Bannerman states, 'there is little doubt that it was in the person of Fergus Mór that the Dalriadic dynasty removed from Ireland to Scotland.' Dàl Riatans may already have been settling there, but this was the significant step in the process, and Bannerman suggests an 'origin myth' was set up around it. A. A. M. Duncan, in *Scotland: Making of the Kingdom*, treats Fergus as a historic figure who did indeed lead the Dàl Riata to Scotland, 'perhaps only shortly before his death'. It remains the case that there is no archaeological evidence for a migration on the scale traditionally ascribed to the one that took place around 500CE. Lloyd and Jenny Laing, while seeming to accept the reality of Fergus, spell out the current thinking:

'Modern opinion favours the view that the "sons" of Fergus were invented to account for an earlier migration to Argyll from Ireland, where Cenel nOengusa [on the islands] was already established before Fergus's time.'

While there must have come a point at which gradual and sporadic small-scale migration from Ulster was formally recognised and organised as a kingdom, there is no definite evidence as to the role and reality of Fergus MacErc.

In Wales, events among the tribes through the fifth and sixth centuries have to be inferred, since the sources are so few. By the end of the period, the tribes or federations recorded in Roman times no longer exist, or continue under a new identity. The likelihood is that the removal of imperial rule and the cessation of the marketing, trading, and industrial economy that accompanied it encouraged a breakup into smaller social units which could each be self-sufficient in food produce and which possessed, or rebuilt, a hillfort for its own security. From here, it could defend its territory, and perhaps from such early beginnings come the land divisions of medieval Wales, the *cantrefi*. *Cantref* means 'a hundred houses', or perhaps 'a hundred hamlets', and is the oldest known subdivision of Welsh territory. The main divisions defined the land occupied by particular tribes, the *gwlad*, or, later, land ruled by a particular chief; thus the *gwlad* ruled by Morgan in the tenth century came to be Glamorgan. It was probably the hierarchical structure of the tribe that encouraged the formation of the *cantref*, as an area under the authority of a subchief. The regularity of size implied by the name was probably less so in reality. It may have had a military purpose, with each *cantref* able to furnish approximately the same number of armed men to the war band. Within his *cantref*, the subchief exercised considerable power, through an assembly of the *uchelwyr*, or leading men, of the district. The *cantref* court, presided over by the subchief, was used to decide on disputes among the free tribesmen: mostly land and boundary matters.

Such a patchwork, especially in the aftermath of monolithic rule, would not be a stable one. Deaths of leaders, the emergence of ambitious strong men, or 'warlords', alliances and attacks, would all make for a shifting pattern, but with a trend towards larger groupings. It was still a largely pagan society, retaining most of the characteristics of 'Celtic' social life already described. From this basis, dynasties developed: royal lineages, which extended their power by intermarriage, by warfare, and by alliance, and by the peaceful absorption of smaller tribal groups for their own protection.

Throughout this period, raids and attempts at colonisation of Wales from Ireland were continuing. The long exposed promontories to north and south were especially vulnerable. In the latter part of the fourth century, an Irish tribe, the Deisi, established themselves in what is now Pembrokeshire. A strong Irish presence existed as far inland as Brecon, where the name recalls the fifth- or sixth-century Irish chief Brychan and his eponymous kingdom of Brycheiniog (Brecknock). Stones carved in the Irish manner, using the Irish ogam alphabet, are found in this area, in the northwest and southwest. Indeed, Wales might have become a Scotland before ever the Scots set up their colony of Dàl Riada far to the north in Pictland, but it seems that the Irish invasions of the north were stemmed. The credit for this has been attributed to a migration by a large section of the Votadini or Gododdin tribe, from the country just north of Hadrian's Wall – their territory, Lothian, was already under pressure from the Angles based at Bamburgh. The leader of this migration, Cunedda, was the grandson of Padarn Pesrut, and was also claimed to be the ancestor of Maelgwn Gwynedd. By tradition, it was Cunedda and his warriors who thrust the Irish back from North Wales. The story is probably a mixture of truth and legend. There is nothing inherently unlikely in the migration: something similar happened several hundred years later, when the Cumbric dynasty of Strathclyde collapsed. But the account of Cunedda's eight sons, each of whom established a royal lineage in different parts of Wales, is a typical myth, comparable to that of Cruithne and his seven sons, supposed founders of seven Pictish kingdoms. Even after invasion attempts died down, Irish settlements, especially in the south, remained as separate enclaves for many generations, and were only gradually absorbed into the developing Welsh kingdoms.

Chapter Eight

Old Religion

The Christian Church was an important element in sustaining the Romano-British communities. From its beginnings in isolated groups of scattered worshippers, the Christian religion had made great advances during the latter years of the third and the early part of the fourth centuries. There was a tenuous structure of British bishoprics. Many of the population still remained pagan or semipagan, but for others there was a faith to defend against the barbarians, as well as a way of life to be valued. Christianity was also established north of the Wall, in the favourable territory of the Novantae. Around 397, St Ninian, returned from a theological education in Rome and perhaps also under St Martin at Tours, founded or joined the church, 'Candida Casa', at Whithorn. It was a bridgehead, a little mission station like those set up in Africa by 19th-century Scottish missionaries.

These earlier missionaries were bringing their new faith to bear against an ancient structure of beliefs, myths, and rituals, accreted over many centuries and firmly embedded in the social life of the people. Fertility, origins, death, and the causes of natural events are the basic subject matter of early religion. Most peoples had their own version of how the world began. The Celtic tribes, as Dr William Ferguson notes in *The Identity of the Scottish Nation*, 'must have had a creation myth but it did not survive the coming of Christianity, for the new learned class, whose business it was to record the truth, would see to that.' Considering how much pagan belief did survive into historic times, this is a surprising statement. Nevertheless, it is true that amongst their preserved legends going back into prehistory, there is hardly anything to indicate what the Celtic peoples thought about the origins of the earth, its gods, and its inhabitants. There are hints that the Old Irish god, Donn, ruler of the dead, was also an ancestor figure, though his role here is inextricably confused with that of the Dagdá, a complex and more powerful deity whose many names include 'Father of All' and 'Red-Eye' (Sun).

But, in common with other ancient cultures, it is virtually certain there was a generally accepted account of how the world and the gods came into being. A tendency to draw the gods into a closer, more human perspective led to the original forms of the major deities being all but forgotten at quite an early time. The great god, Lug, for example, whose name survives in such river names as the English Lugg and the Scottish Luggie, as well as in the Lughnasa festival, began as a personification of the sun, as the meaning of his name, 'brightness', testifies – a very important god. The sun plays a vital part in many creation myths. But, in the mythology of early Ireland, Lug was brought much closer to the Gaels' own time, as chief of the Tuatha dé Danann, and the father, albeit a supernatural one, of the hero Fionn mac Cumhaill and, in some tales, of Cuchulainn. It remains surprising that, among peoples with a trained priestly cadre, a creation myth should not have survived.

It does not seem that there ever was a pantheon of Celtic gods, to be compared with the divine assemblages of ancient Greece, based on Mount Olympus, or of the Norse peoples with Valhalla. Despite many changes over the generations, and varying accounts, these collections of deities have a certain consistency and their domestic arrangement is not very different from that of a mortal ruling dynasty. By contrast, the surviving information on the Celtic gods suggests that they were viewed and understood in a completely different way. Originally impersonal forces and presences, sun, moon, sky, water, earth, and always retaining some of the impersonality and strength of these elemental aspects, they also were, from a very early time, identified with the two great human preoccupations of fertility/reproduction and death. From the Irish legends, the prime source of information, it would appear that female deities were of great, perhaps supreme, importance at first. Ana or Anu, the name meaning 'abundance', is often identified by scholars as the tribal god figure named in the Tuatha dé Danann (see Chapter Ten) and, despite her name, she also had a malevolent aspect. Ana is also identified with the land, though, in Irish legend, she has numerous rivals in this respect, including Ernmas, a mother figure among gods, just as she has rivals in her charge over fertility, including the similar-sounding Áine. Ernmas is also seen as the mother of the war-goddess, or Morrigan ('great queen'), though this role in warfare is shared with the goddesses Badb and Macha in a typical three-part set. In the different tellings, these names often appear to be manifestations of essentially the same deity. Among male deities, the Dagda, mentioned above, is also identified with the Tuatha dé Danann, but his skills, as described, are human-related ones, to do with craft and proficiency in warfare; very like those of Lug.

The corresponding figure to Anu in Welsh myth is Dôn, a mother figure whose children all play important parts in ancient legends of Welsh origins. Both Wales and Ireland preserve accounts of a world of the dead, presided over by its own divinity: Donn in Ireland had his house, Tech Duinn, at the western tip of the Beare peninsula. Arawn in Wales was the lord of Annwn, though originally he shared the role with a less benign figure, Hafgan. Annwn was a mysterious location, in some texts said to be underground or undersea; in others it becomes Caer Siddi, a great revolving castle surrounded by the sea.

While the Roman gods were absent figures who could, and needed to, be represented by a priesthood (Julius Caesar like many eminent Romans was a *flamen*, or initiated priest), the islanders' gods, at least as described later in the written accounts, were very often present themselves, in human form. In Wales, too, the Celtic god, Belenus, equated with the Greek Apollo, appears in the *Mabinogi* as *Beli Mawr*, Beli the Great, an actively procreative ancestral figure (his name also appears in the first-century British leader Cunobelin, 'hound of Belenus'). Considering the importance of mistletoe in the druidic cult, as described by the Roman Pliny in his first-century *Natural History*, professor Venceslas Kruta writes, in *The Celts of the West*, that:

> ' . . . it was almost certainly a particularly important ritual pertaining to a cult associated with one of the greatest Celtic gods; it is hardly surprising that mistletoe was considered to have magical virtue, for, because it is perennial, it is to the tree what the soul is to the body. For this reason it was regarded as a direct emanation of the god in person.'

This god, Kruta says, has not been identified, though he himself relates it to a man-headed horse figure found in some continental artefacts and coins. Rather oddly, he says this creature is unknown in Europe, outside the Celtic world, though a certain resemblance to a centaur seems clear enough. Because so little is known about the gods of the continental Celts and their connections with those of the British Isles peoples, speculation is inevitable. Kruta seems on firmer ground when he notes, of the Celtic goddesses, that they 'were probably descended from the mythology of the first farming people'. Fertility, animal care, and childbirth are the prime attributes of these goddesses.

There is ample evidence on the ground that early inhabitants, from the latter part of the Neolithic Age and into the Bronze Age, were very much preoccupied by death. Their grave monuments, houses of the dead, were much larger and more imposing than the houses of the living. The cairns and chambered tombs remain to show that death was treated with portentous awe. Enormous energy and thousands of man-hours went into the making of these funeral sites. But, by the early centuries CE, whether or not beliefs had changed, certainly the business of

burial had become far less of a massive undertaking. Most
Pictish burial sites, for example, consist of long cists, a shallow
rectangular grave lined with stone slabs, suggesting that bodies
were buried rather than cremated. Some of the cist burials are
grouped and covered by an earth platform to form a low barrow,
and often Pictish symbol stones have been found in association
with these. These unelaborate graves suggest a more matter-of-
fact view of death, but there may be other explanations of which
we know nothing. In other areas, disposal of the dead may have
been by exposure on open wooden platforms, followed by
burning or scattering of the bones. As a general intellectual or
spiritual trend, one can see a movement from the earth-based
religious outlook represented by the stone and earthen tombs,
to a sky-centred view in which prime deities were related to the
sun and moon. The view of the nature of an afterlife probably
changed in accompaniment.

Rather more is known about the relationship of religious
belief and the preoccupation with fertility. Before the conversion
of the Celtic-speaking peoples to Christianity, their kings had a
dual role, as war leaders and as prime figures in the religious life
of their people. The evidence for this is extensive, though almost
entirely from sources and commentaries relating to the tribes of
Gaul and of Roman Britain and to the Gaels of Ireland. While it
may reasonably be supposed that the functions of North British
(Strathclyde) and Pictish kings were similar, it may equally well
be supposed that there were significant differences. The mystical
functions of a king are likely to be more ancient than his military
or administrative ones, stemming from the fundamental preoccupation of early society with the fertility of soil, animals, and
people. Kings were originally intermediaries between the people
and the forces controlling life: they reigned for a year and were
sacrificed, their blood spilt to ensure regeneration. Later, they
survived until old age or physical debility required their removal
and replacement. Some time before the first century CE, in Celtic
and other societies, individual kings had made themselves more

durable, though variants of the sacrifice ritual long continued, and a more elaborate system of mediation between people and nature had evolved. In *The Celts of the West*, Venceslas Kruta notes how 'the ideal sovereign, as described in the written documents, was supposed to ensure a perfect climate, a temperature and rainfall favourable to vegetation, an abundance of livestock and good harvests, an absence of vermin and disease, peace and respect for law.' This was a tall order, even for the luckiest of kings, and no doubt scapegoats and explanations were needed when all did not attain to the ideal. In the ancient Irish tradition, the king quite explicitly married the land, in a ceremony that can be traced far back in other traditions too; it is recorded for example in a Sumerian hymn of the second millennium BCE. The semimythical king Niall Noígiallach, of the fourth century CE, as told in *Echtra MacnEchach Muigmedóin*, 'The Adventure of the Sons of Eochaid Mugmedón', slept reluctantly with an old hag who waylaid him. In the morning, she had changed into the radiant beautiful girl, Sovereignty, thus confirming his (and his descendants') kingship. Among the Celtic-speaking islanders, this priestly connection between king and soil was long maintained, even after Christianity had become universal. The twelfth-century Welsh traveller, Giraldus Cambrensis, described, with some revulsion, the coronation ceremony of a subking of an Ulster tribe. A white mare was brought forward, with which the king carried out a symbolic copulation. The mare was then slaughtered, skinned, and boiled. The king was immersed in the warm broth, and then he and those present ate the meat and drank the broth.

Among the pre-Christian Celtic tribes, this cultic system was maintained and applied by a particular order of society, the druids. They were a high-status group recruited from among the noble families. In some cases, a king might himself be a druid, which implies that he had gone through the 20-year training required to make a young man or woman proficient in the knowledge and skills of the order. Even without this exceptional preparation, a member of a king's *derbfine* would be likely to know what was required of a king when he participated in the rites of the druids' oak grove, or in casting offerings to a sacred pool or stream, or in examining omens and auspices.

Druidical training's lengthy process perhaps weeded out those of insufficient learning or judgment but was also necessary, since much of their knowledge was preserved orally and required to be committed to memory. Although the oral tradition is, normally and, no doubt, rightly, seen as conservative in its effects, maintaining a fixed orthodoxy through many generations, the cult clearly underwent changes, and what is said of druidical practice in first-century Gaul is not likely to be entirely true of fourth-century Ireland or Pictland. The Greek Christian writer, Hippolytus (third century) noted that the Celtic druids eagerly took up the study of Pythagoras's teachings, brought to them after the master's death by a slave of his. The mystic and divinatory qualities of Pythagoras doubtless appealed to the druids, but its acceptance shows that they were open to the ideas of others, at least when these were congenial or conformed to basic principles.

Most of what information there is on the druids' cults is given by foreign and often hostile reporters and should be treated with due care. Classical writers sought to make sense of the 'uncivilised' world by reducing it to their own terms whenever possible. Thus, Strabo records that the druids, 'in addition to natural philosophy, also study moral philosophy'. Caesar notes that 'they hold many discussions as touching the stars and their movements, the size of the universe and the earth, the order of nature, the strength and power of the immortal gods.' This was the stuff of all ancient philosophy, and the content of the druidical discussions is not recorded. Nevertheless, a degree of respect for the druids' intellectual powers and range of thought is evident. They are not considered at the level at which, say, 19th-century explorers tended to place the African 'witch doctor'. But the prevalence of human sacrifice in the first two centuries CE, if not later, is plain:

'Their predilection for human sacrifice is incontestable, and the descriptions of the great wicker-work images which were filled with men and animals and then set on fire is reminiscent of the descriptions in the early Irish tales of the trapping of heroes in the *bruidne*, the so-called hostelries, and the subsequent burning of these.'

So wrote Dr Anne Ross in *Pagan Celtic Britain*. Dr Nora Chadwick takes a more restrained view in *The Celts*, suggesting that such holocausts were rare, and probably related to times of extreme tension. The first-century Roman poet, Lucan, set out to make his readers' flesh creep with descriptions of the reeking altars and bloody groves of the druids, where bodies and parts of bodies hung in trees as propitiation to savage deities. His contemporary, Pliny, referred in the *Natural History* to Britain as being 'spellbound by magic and conducts so much ritual that it would seem that it was Britain that had given magic to the Persians'.

The Romans never sought to understand the basis of Celtic beliefs, and could see the Celtic gods only in relation to their own Graeco-Roman pantheon. By the later fifth century, it is likely that human sacrifice was very little practised by the Caledonians or the Scots. Such things would have been even more abhorrent to Christians than were other heathen practices but, though Columba remonstrated – to little avail – against such still-current pagan notions as the universal habit of looking for omens in everything, none of the early saints seems to have had cause to fulminate against druidic sacrifices. How far there was still a cultic significance in the decapitation of bodies is unclear. Christianity did not put a stop to this, any more than it did to warfare in general. The Celtic tribes were head-hunters, and while this may bring the word 'barbarian' back in a rush, it does not seem that lopping off heads was a nondiscriminating activity. The desired heads were those of enemies defeated in battle, which were exhibited at the victorious warrior's door, and also – before Christianity – in the druidic sanctuary. The many representations of human heads found in Celtic archaeological sites in Britain, Ireland, and Europe testify to the fact that the head was venerated. As Anne Ross points out, this was not just a Celtic practice, but:

'They are however singular in the extent to which they carried this veneration, incorporating the head in their art and in their religious practices as a symbol and as an object of superstitious regard.'

She also draws attention to the continuing links of wells with severed heads in the Highlands and Islands (and might also have mentioned, in connection with the burning of groups of men in 'hostelries', the numerous later accounts of burnings of people in towers, churches, and inns during the 16th and 17th centuries, as a result of blood feuds between clans). Many people have noted the remarkable pediment of the twelfth-century Romanesque doorway of Clonfert Cathedral, Co. Galway, whose array of carved heads looks almost exactly as one might suppose a warrior's head shrine to appear. It may be a unique example of archaism, preserving a pre-Christian aspect of the site.

There is a certain duality in these recorded fragments of the druidic cult. On one hand, there is the abstract and spiritual concept of the transmigration of souls, the evidence of study of 'moral philosophy', and the recorded triadic precept of 'Worship the gods; do no evil; be manly in conduct'; on the other, there is the bloody business of sacrificial disembowelling and the examining of entrails, as well as the holocausts of prisoners trapped in their wicker baskets. Did the same druids officiate in both? There is a strong sense here of a struggle between primitive and modernising beliefs. The event of the Roman invasion, and the fear of its extension to Ireland, may have played a part in reinvigorating the more brutal and antique aspects of the cult. The role of the druids in celebrating the great seasonal feasts is accepted, but how far they maintained the cult of individual gods is not clear. The wider organisation of the druids, at any time, is not known. In the last century BCE, Julius Caesar reported that their main centre was in Britain. Whether this represents a removal from Gaul to a safer place in the face of Roman invasion, or a cult with its roots in Britain, which has spread to the continent, is equally unclear. In the first and second centuries, the island of Môn (Anglesey) had been the centre of the druidic cult of the British and it seems also of the Gaulish tribes. One of Tacitus's most dramatic passages records the destruction of this centre by the Romans under Suetonius Paulinus:

'On the shore stood the opposing army with its dense array of armed warriors while between the ranks dashed women in black attire like the Furies, with hair dishevelled, waving brands. All around, the druids lifting up their hands to heaven and pouring forth dreadful imprecations, scared our soldiers by the unfamiliar sight, so that, as if their limbs were paralysed, they stood motionless, exposing themselves to wounds. Then urged by their general's appeal and mutual encouragements not to quail before a troop of frenzied women, they bore the standards onwards, smote down all resistance, and wrapped the enemy in the flames of his own burning brands. A force was next set over the conquered, and their groves, devoted to inhuman superstitions, were destroyed. They deemed it, indeed, a duty to cover their altars with the blood of captives and to consult their deities through human entrails.'

After that we hear no more of a 'capital' of druidism, though the cult itself continued until its gradual absorption into Christianity. By the fourth century, in the time of the first missionary saints, there was a vast body of druidical learning and lore and, although references are made to druids' books, it seems most likely that the great bulk of this was taught by rote and committed to memory, in the same way that the Indian Vedic hymns were preserved (with great accuracy) for centuries. There is nothing to suggest that there was an archdruid in later times and, if the way in which the Christian Church was organised is a guide, then each provincial kingdom, with its group of *tuatha*, would have had its own druids, members of its own leading families. Druids had the right to move between kingdoms, as did bards, and thus had opportunities to confer, and, no doubt, often acted as ambassadors or emissaries (see below). The profound conservatism built into the system by their training process was a guard against innovation or heresy, though it is very unlikely that heresy was a concept of theirs. It was not a cult that demanded fervent faith or abstract love, or that set a moral code. The notions of sin and retribution seem scarcely to have been present. Despite the placing of the hero-champion at the peak of achievement, they were not individualists; this is also seen in their law codes, where the tribe or kindred always took responsibility for a single member's action. Such a collective spirit does not accord well with the doctrine of personal salvation and helps to explain why the Gaels had difficulty in accepting the notion of hell. Julius Caesar noted that the Gauls believed in the transmigration of souls, and all the evidence of texts and grave sites shows that they certainly believed in an afterlife.

The hero stories of ancient Ireland record a particular form of fatedness, in the concept of *geis* (*geassa* in modern Irish). This was usually a kind of taboo, or ban, placed upon particular individuals, forbidding them from doing a certain action. More rarely, it was a positive requirement to perform some deed. It is related to the practice of magic, and the spell or incantation that places a charm on someone, and which cannot be broken without damaging results. Druids could perceive such fatedness in individuals, but had no power to avert or defeat it. Often such a bond is placed on a warrior by a woman, as with Deirdre and Naîsi, or Brían and his stepmother in the story of the well at the world's end. In the finest stories, *geis* is like the tragic fate of Greek hero tales. It may compel a hero to do great deeds, with tragic consequences for himself. There is no escape from it. Its existence outside the realm of legend is shown by the restrictions placed on early kings. Far from being free agents able to exercise their power as they pleased, these rulers were hemmed in by prescriptive *geis*. The king of Tara should not lie in bed and allow the sun to rise above him. The king of Ulster was forbidden to drink the waters of Lough Swilly at sunset. Such prohibitions are linked to the priestly status of the king in pre-Christian religion.

The druids' cult retained its preoccupation with fertility, and a keen sense of the living Earth, not in the Gaian or superecological sense of today, but in terms of natural features being animated by spirits that lived as the stream, hill, or field itself, but could also have an identity given to them, often that of an animal. So certain streams might be 'bull streams', certain lochs 'horse lochs'. These identities remain fossilised in such names as Kanturk ('boar's head') or Loch Eck ('horse'). There is ample evidence from British and Irish sites that tribute was paid to these watery spirits of place, by casting precious objects into the water. In fact, just as animal sacrificers, though offering the beast to the god, usually ate the meat and left the bones for the deity, many of the more routine offerings may have been weapons and utensils somewhat past their best. Often they were broken, though the breaking may have been part of the ritual. But some, like the splendid bronze shield of the first or second century CE, found in the Thames at Battersea, were of very fine workmanship, expensive items never meant for practical use but intended as votive objects.

More than 400 names of deities worshipped by the Celtic-speaking peoples of Europe and the British Isles have been identified, most of them, as Nora Chadwick points out, found only once; and even the more frequently found names tend to be restricted to a particular region. In Romanised Gaul and south Britain, many names were carved in stone at sacred sites; in Ireland, many have been preserved in the oral tradition that was ultimately written down. North of Hadrian's Wall, where writing seems to have been unknown or very rare until the fifth century, there are no inscriptions. Not one of these names comes from Scotland. Our ignorance of Pictish mythology leaves only the Pictish carved stones, certain place names, and archaeological finds to offer clues to the gods and goddesses of the Picts. It is reasonable to suppose that their cult shared the general characteristics of that of their southern neighbours. Within the same overall seasonal pattern, which determined most of their forms of ritual, it seems that many tribes had their own specific deities. On the other hand, the broad types of god, goddess, or spirit seem to have shared many similarities among the peoples, as Anne Ross demonstrates in the pages of *Pagan Celtic Britain*, and some of these resemblances remained constant over considerable periods of time.

Some scanty evidence is found in Scottish place names. Among the most intriguing of these are those which indicate the location of a druidic centre in the form of a scared grove, or *nemeton*: a Gallic-Brittonic word identified by Stuart Piggott as related to Latin *nemus*, grove, or clearing within a grove; and so a word of Indo-European origin. Such names occur across a very wide zone from *Medionemeton*, a location recorded as being close to the Antonine Wall in Scotland, to *Drunemeton* in Galatia. It crops up in the numerous Nymptons of Devon as well as Navity and Rosneath in Scotland; the Old Irish word *nemed*, sanctuary, is clearly related. Most identifiably Pictish place names refer to landscape features and to land divisions. But a number of river names, such as Dee and Don (both indicative of a divinity) and Nethy (indicative of purity) suggest a cult connection. In his pamphlet, *The Picts and Their Place Names*, Dr Bill Nicolaisen looks at reasons for supposing that Aber- names may indicate something more than a river mouth or confluence, perhaps denoting the cultic significance of such a place. The names of Arbuthnot, which preserves both aber- and a river name which notes healing qualities, and Aberfeldy, which preserves that of a *pellaidh*, or water spirit, show plain connections with the supernatural. Some of Scotland's numerous -tarff ('bull') place names are also Pictish in origin. Nearly all of these are water names, showing that the Picts found the same inspiration in water sites as did the Brigantians and other tribes of Britain and Gaul. Even in the 17th century, bulls were being sacrificed on an island in Loch Maree, which was deemed to be especially sacred, as it was itself in a tiny loch set within a larger island on the great loch. The large number of bull carvings – more than 30, of which only six remain – found at Burghead, in Moray, have strongly suggested that it was a centre for a bull cult in pagan times. Among the many sacred animals and birds of the islanders, the bull undoubtedly occupied an important position. Irish legend, too, with its many tales and episodes linked to the 'Cattle Raid of Cooley', help to bear this out, though bull-related place names are rarer than in Scotland – Clontarf is one of the few. The bull had clear associations with fertility and power, but also with divination. In the Irish *tarbhfeis*, 'bull ceremony', a chosen man ate the meat and broth of a new-killed bull and slept while four druids chanted above him. The purpose was to find, in his dream, the name of the next to be king. Long into the Common Era, a bull's hide was reputed to have supernatural powers. In a ritual very like the *tarbhfeis*, when a community had an important question to resolve, one of its members would be wrapped in the still-hot hide of a newly killed ox and sent to pass a night in a cave or by a waterfall; by the end of this procedure, known as *taghairm*, he would have the right answer. This was only one of a host of folk ways preserved among the Gaels from druidical times.

There is some sparse archaeological evidence of local bull cults. The discovery of a collection of bull carvings at and near the Pictish coastal fort at Burghead has led to speculation of such a cult there. Scotland and Ireland, in general, have been much less fruitful sources of actual pagan Celtic cult objects than south Britain and continental Europe; and much of the tribes' religious practice can only be inferred. Of course, many cult objects would have been carved out of wood, with a much lower chance of survival, though one or two striking wooden items have been found from pre-Pictish times, like the five-foot-high female idol figure found near Ballachulish in Argyll and dated to the early centuries CE.

Water, both still and running, played an important part in mythology and religion. Lakes, wells and waterways were seen as having their own protective deities, to be worshipped and propitiated. Many were later attached to saints' names. Of the more than 200 holy wells in Wales, the most celebrated is St Winifred's. Its legend is a Christian one, but showing pre-Christian elements. The story is of the holy maiden, Winifred, niece of St Beuno (sixth century), whose beauty attracted the prince Caradog. When she resisted his advances, in rage he cut her head off. For his action he was struck dead, but Beuno followed Winifred's head, where it had rolled down the hill, retrieved it, reattached it to her body, and she came back to life. Where the head had come to rest, a spring welled up, with wonderful healing properties. Although Christian pilgrims are only recorded from the twelfth century, there is a strong suggestion of an earlier pagan head cult linked to the tutelary spirit of the spring.

The tribes of the British Isles dwelt, as the modern inhabitants still do, among the monuments of ancient predecessors. But, without the vastly greater population, the tamed countryside, and the residential sprawl of today, these monuments were far more apparent. While this was especially true for certain places, most notably in middle Ireland, in Wessex, and for the Orcadians and the inhabitants of west Lewis, who had Brogar, Stenness, and Callanish (not yet enveloped in the rising peat) to gaze at, there were many hundreds of stone circles throughout the country, often close to imposing burial mounds. Whatever their original purpose, it is likely that some of these were adapted to forms of worship presided over by the druids, even if it was only by providing a sacred site. It would seem likely that the stone circles were at no time regarded as alien constructions but as a 'heritage', part of the living tradition. Many generations on, a tall stone, at Meigle in the former Pictland, with Bronze Age cup marks on its base would be used in the eighth century as a Christian cross-slab.

CHAPTER NINE

New Religion

Faced with this great hedge of cultic beliefs, superstitions, and practices, the Christian pioneers had one or two important weapons. The chief one was their religion's in-built urge to evangelise, to spread the gospel news and make others believe it with the same intensity as themselves. Unlike the mystery religions with which it at first competed, Christianity was not exclusive; it was open to anyone who accepted its teaching, slave or aristocrat, Celt or Scythian. Such a drive was foreign to the druidic cult, which was formed out of customary procedures and which, shared by the whole population, had no need to proselytise. For the same reason, it had had no cause to defend itself. It had never been attacked before and its passivity made it vulnerable, like some lumbering herbivore suddenly confronted by a new and sharp-toothed species. Vastly outnumbered as they were, the missionaries knew that other populations had been won over; moreover, since the time of Constantine the Great, the Roman Empire had officially adopted Christianity (apart from the brief reign of Julian). Though collapsed in the west, the empire was still mighty in the east. This may or may not have helped the cause, but the prestige it brought was undeniable. The Latin liturgy and the communion ceremony were rich in mystique. Christianity could not be ignored.

In another respect the missionaries had an advantage over the druids. Ironically, they were the inheritors of much classical pagan knowledge and educational technique, passed on by and learned from the Greeks, whose colony towns could be found from Marseilles to the Black Sea. They had some understanding of the art of rhetoric, of disputation and the presentation of argument. The druids had no such linguistic structures to defend their position. But intellectual arguments rarely win converts and, in the one recorded confrontation of saint and druid, between Columcille and Broichan, in Adamnan's life of the saint, it is Columba's superior magic, not his debating skill, that wins the day. Miracles are ascribed to most of the Celtic saints, and they played important roles as averters of evil. Perhaps because he had been a figure hitherto missing from people's lives, the saints took to the devil in a strong way. St Serf had a conversation with him in a cave on the Fife coast. Even on the holy isle of Iona, St Columba had to take precautions against an evil spirit lodged in a milk pail. But at that time the spirits and the icons of paganism were still very much present, deeply lodged in popular belief and imagination. Centuries later, some of them would still figure in Pictish stone-carving, like the horned Cernunnos figure at Meigle.

Still, the religion of peace, of humility, of 'love thy neighbour', and 'turn the other cheek', of renunciation of worldly things, of original sin and the need for atonement, cannot have been easy to incorporate into a society founded on a basis of rank, conspicuous display, slavery, and armed raiding. The Britons, Picts, and Irish, however, saw things from their own standpoint. In the fourth century, at the 'Alleluia Battle', the Picts had a chance to note the efficacy of the Christian god as a war leader, and the Old Testament supplied ample further evidence of this. Asceticism and the monastic life clearly had appeal to many people; sometimes, in forms of the most austere and solitary sort, in the beehive huts of Hebridean isles and islets, found as far away as North Rona, over the Atlantic horizon. Eventually, with the conversion through the seventh and eighth centuries of the Anglo-Saxons and of the Franks,

Christianity and the Latin language would be of practical value in providing links and conduits, enabling contact with other peoples and kingdoms. But this had nothing to do with the original acceptance of the new religion.

Though it had its mysteries and roles reserved to the priesthood, Christianity was an open cult, in that its basic story and its moral teachings were closely linked to each other and available to all believers. It was with the advent of the new religion that the priestly class consented to the passing on of knowledge in writing. In Ireland, a unique script was developed, whose use spread to Irish communities in Scotland and South Wales. This was ogam, and seems to have been devised in order to be incised in stone or wood; it is often found on edges and margins. Its 20 symbols, later increased to 25, employ only straight lines. They correspond to the letters of the Latin alphabet, and each was given the name of a tree as its identifier. The earliest ogam inscriptions are found from the third century, and it remained in use until the eighth. Over 300 survive, most consisting of no more than a name or names. It was not intended for continuous prose, or for use with the quill.

By 431CE, Christian communities already existed in Ireland, and their presence was known in Rome. In this year, the Latin chronicler, Prosper, records that pope Celestine sent one Palladius to be a bishop to those Irish Christians. At this time, the Pelagian heresy was rife among the British Christians and Palladius, a staunch anti-Pelagian, was probably commissioned to keep it out of Ireland, as well as to minister to the faithful, rather than evangelise among the pagan tribes. His area of activity is most likely to have been Leinster, the province most obviously open to influences from southern Britain and the European continent, but his achievement has been dimmed by that of Patrick, who was an evangelist first and foremost. We have his own word for this: he went to spread the Gospel among pagans *usque ubi nemo ultra est*, 'as far as where there is no one to be found' (the *Confession*). Born in a Romano-British

community, son of a deacon, grandson of a priest, he was kid-
napped in an Irish slave raid at 16, escaped after six years, and
was inspired by a sense of divine mission to return as a missionary. His area of activity was in the north, and it is most
unlikely that he was the only evangelist at work. Other early
saints, Ailbe, Déclán, and Ciarán among them, have been traditionally identified as contemporary with or even preceding
him. The only sure thing about Patrick's dates is that he lived in
the fifth century. He did not die in a Christian Ireland; the process of conversion was a long and sporadic one, and was not
complete until around the end of the sixth century. In that
process, much of what had been pagan religion was imported,
in a Christianised form, into the new cult. In Ireland as elsewhere, Christian churches were erected on, or in close proximity to, sites of pagan worship and ritual; Armagh close to Emain
Macha is the prime but far from the only example. Holy wells
and other significant sites were transferred from the control of
tutelary spirits to that of saints. The most spectacular example
of the transference of ancient belief is in St Brigid, at her centre
of Kildare, the second part of whose name, from *dara*, oak, suggests druidic links. Around the historical, if hazy, Brigid, first
abbess of Kildare, who died around 525CE, has accumulated
much of the lore attached to an earlier Brigid or Brid, a powerful goddess, daughter of the Dagdá, whose attributes of fire and
fertility made her a central figure in popular veneration.

However little, more is known about St Patrick, who went
from Britain to Ireland, than about those who made the journey in the other direction after his death (with the great exception of St Columba). Marjorie Anderson remarked 'there is
hardly an Irish saint associated with Scotland in the sixth century for whom the evidence is more than barely admissible'.
Even with St Ninian, despite his reputation, there is no real
evidence as to his life span, his education, and his achievements. St Kentigern's origin, though furnished with many
accurate local details, is a legendary tale. The details and

impressions that we have of men like these come from life stories written in their praise centuries later and, though they may incorporate authentic details from manuscripts now lost, there is no way of telling. The sainthood of Celtic clerics was neither awarded nor confirmed by the Bishop of Rome in his Lateran Palace. It was the verdict of their contemporaries and followers. Their familiar names suggest a sort of proprietorial affection among the people for some of these pioneers. Grand Kentigern, founder of the Church at Glasgow, whose name means 'great lord', was also known as Mungo, 'dear one'. St Luoc, St Laise, and others had the qualifier *mo*-placed in front of their personal names, with the sense of 'dear' or 'dear little', still preserved in place names like Kilmoluag and Lamlash.

Whatever the true facts of Ninian's story may be, archaeology has confirmed the existence of an ancient church at the site of Ninian's Candida Casa, 'white house', at Whithorn (which itself is from the Anglian words meaning 'white house') and other Christian sites, from around 500CE. Christianity was established in this area soon after, or perhaps even before, the Romans left, though only in isolated pockets. Its first practitioners may have been simply Christian merchants or farmers, rather than missionary evangelists. From such nuclei the new faith spread among the Britons, though the twelfth-century Life of Kentigern, by Jocelyn of Furness, says that their first Christian king, Rhyderch, in the late sixth century, was baptised in Ireland, and that he subsequently summoned Kentigern (who was of the Gododdin rather than the Strathclyde Britons) from Wales, to where he had removed himself. In his study, *Medieval Wales*, David Walker points out that 'All this could be legend, rather than fact . . . No ancient dedication has been claimed for him.'

A number of writers have noted that it is curious that Ninian, with his base in the extreme southwest of Scotland, should be associated chiefly with missionary work up the east coast, although he, as, apparently, a bishop, not an abbot, was

not tied down to any one monastery, and Jocelyn also notes
that Ninian had formed a Christian community in Glasgow,
long before Kentigern. Despite the many St Ninian dedica-
tions, Dr Kathleen Hughes noted:

> ' . . . there is no early evidence to show that the commemo-
> rations to Ninian in Pictland are early, and since the form of
> his name in such commemorations is either latinised or in a
> Gaelic form derived through Scots vernacular the com-
> memorations may go back only to a later development of his
> cult.'

That could mean the twelfth century, when Aelred's *Life of
Ninian* was written and interest in the saint was clearly high.

In Wales, as in Ireland and Scotland, the 'dark ages' were
also the age of the saints. The actual way in which Christianity
spread across the country is often obscure, though ably traced
by Sian Victory in *The Celtic Church in Wales*. The kingdoms of
Wales did not lose touch with developments on the continent
of Europe. The western seaways remained an open route and
were as important as they had always been as a conduit of culture and ideas. Following the establishment of monasteries
there, Ireland, in turn, became a source of missionary effort.
There are many evidences of this in Wales, not least those
saints descended from Brychan and associated with places in
the centre and south. The cult of Brigid or Brid was early
brought to Wales in the form of St Ffraid. Then again, memories of the empire died slowly in Wales, and the prestige of
Christianity as the religion of Constantine the Great was a
valuable asset. When northern Europe, and much of the territory of south Britain, was overrun by pagans, Christianity,
even if it seemed to have failed to protect them, was one of the
means by which the Britons could show their difference to the
invaders. Above all, perhaps, there was a steady supply of dedicated and intrepid men prepared to bring the Gospel message
to every part of the old tribal lands. Pious, austere, inspired,

they set personal examples of unworldliness, asceticism, and charity. It was of their Church that the French historian Ernest Renan wrote:

> 'Few forms of Christianity have offered an ideal of Christian perfection as pure as the Celtic Church of the sixth, seventh and eighth centuries. Nowhere, perhaps, has God been better worshipped in spirit.' (*Etudes d'Histoire Réligieuse*)

Many of the Welsh missionaries themselves became closely identified with a single region, district, or even parish. It is to this that Wales owes its many hundreds of Llan- names, the great majority denoting the church founded by, or dedicated to, a particular saintly person. The evangelist who has emerged with greatest distinction is, of course, St David, whose church at remote Menevia has become Wales's prime cathedral. David is a figure of whom little is known and, though many churches are dedicated to him throughout the south, this may be a result of the twelfth-century efforts to promote the independence of the Welsh Church. Many others were also active. Padarn, bearer of a name with some resonance in tribal history, established the church at Llanbadarn Fawr and linked up with the Irish or Irish-descended missionaries coming out of Breichyniog. A great Roman villa took on a new identity when St Illtud established his church and school by its site; it is still known as Llantwit Major. Further west and into the hills, St Teilo founded the church at Llandeilo Fawr. In the north, one of the chief moving spirits was St Beuno; his centre was at Clynnog Fawr but he or his followers penetrated right into Anglesey and along the northeast coastal strip. There is regrettably little contemporary information. Even the seventh-century *Life of St Samson*, still preserved, though it confirms some names such as that of Illtud, has almost nothing in the way of historical detail. Authors of the lives of saints were not concerned to record history; their aim was to magnify the spiritual impact of their subject and, consequently, there are more

miracles than facts to be found in these texts. The procedure
of the evangelists was usually to establish a monastery, a little
ecclesiastical settlement with a church, dwelling huts, and the
necessary farm sheds. From this centre, trained monks could
go out and establish churches as daughter foundations.

Because of its isolation, the Church in Wales, as in Ireland
and Scotland, took a distinctive form. Its origins lay in the tiny
self-seeding cells of Christians in Romano-British communities. Before the collapse of Rome, bishops had gone from
Britain to attend conclaves in Europe. While over much of Europe the Church was stifled, here on the edge it flourished.
Naturally enough, with no outside influences to shape it, it took
a form that aligned it with the structure of society. Here too,
bishops were often also abbots, and tended to be men of high
social rank. Spiritual responsibilities and ecclesiastical contacts
were combined with the role of royal advisers and diplomats.
With a corps of monks trained in writing and decorating parch-
ment scripts, the abbeys became repositories of historical records. A consequence of this was a sundering of the bards and the
bardic tradition. In pre-Christian days, bards and druids had
complementary and, often, overlapping functions. The orders
in which they were ranked indicated a unity of structure. A
strong poetic tradition developed within the Church and, since
panegyric and praise had been important aspects of the poetic
repertoire, these transferred naturally to the writing of hymns.
But a strong pagan and secular tradition also remained among
the bards. In the pre-Christian community, their skill with
words was closely allied to magic, and the power of satire and
cursing was something personal and integral to their role as
bards. They were loath to give this privileged role up to the
priests of the new order. There was rivalry between bards and
priests. Maelgwn Gwynedd, the king reviled by Gildas for his
tepid attitude to religion, may have had the bard Taliesin as his
chief bard; and Taliesin was later renowned for insisting on the
prophetic, magus-like role of the bard:

'These are Taliesin's rimes,
These shall live to distant times,
And the bard's prophetic rage
Animate a future age.'

One of the few saints known to give honour and status to the
secular bards was Columba. In Christian Gaelic society, the
bards, or *filí*, were a resentful and disruptive element, and it
was proposed that they should be exiled or even put beyond
the law. Perhaps because of his own early training and personal
accomplishment in bardic skills, the great abbot prevailed over
the abolishers, and it was established that each *tuath* should
have its own resident *ollamh*, or supreme poet and professor of
letters, with an honoured place, and the opportunity to teach
students. This was a significant step in the preservation of
popular and traditional culture.

How widely and deeply Christianity spread among the
ordinary people is impossible to say. The Celtic Church, in its
Irish, Pictish, and British forms, may not have been a religion
of the 'masses', but may, like the druidic cult that preceded it,
rather have been essentially the preserve of the upper ranks
(though St Patrick was as willing to convert slaves as chiefs, it
does not follow that each played similar parts). The number of
churches specifically mentioned in Pictland during the time of
the Pictish kingdoms is small. A. B. Scott, a fervent Pictophile,
was able to identify 28, some of them on very late and hazy
evidence. W. F. Skene maps 13 churches in the same area prior
to the eighth century. The churches themselves were generally
built of wood, or wattle and daub, and were very small. Their
purpose was for monks and priests to sing their offices and cel-
ebrate the Mass for themselves and perhaps a few privileged
lay people. Preaching was an activity for outdoors. It is most
likely to have been at a temporary outside altar that the common people were given communion, on an infrequent basis,
coinciding with church festivals and local saints' days.

Later writers have given the name of the 'Celtic Church' to the Christian organisation that arose in Ireland, Scotland, and Wales, and, until the domination of Canterbury, in England. As with all things Celtic in the British Isles, this name was never used or considered at the time, and its later bestowal may cast a false sense of unity and identity on what always was a community of independent churches, sharing fundamental beliefs and preserving links with the Church elsewhere, but with no corporate hierarchy or head.

In a way that suggests continuity with the druidic cult, the Celtic church's organisation corresponded to that of the tribal areas. Each of these, except perhaps for very small groups, had its bishop, who was able to consecrate new priests. This spiritual role, and his place in the apostolic succession deriving ultimately from St Peter, gave the bishop an aura of holiness. But, in any area where there was an abbey, the most visibly and politically important cleric was not a bishop but the abbot. The abbot was normally a member of a royal family and thus very much involved in the maintaining of that royal line and in the family's administration of its kingdom. Sometimes, as with Finnian at Clonard, the role of bishop and abbot seemes to have been combined. Late in the Pictish kingdom, an abbot might not be a cleric at all, like Crinan, the layman who bore the title abbot of Dunkeld, and who married the daughter of king Malcolm II and was father of king Duncan. Less is known about Celtic abbesses, but they too could be persons of note, like Darlugdach, abbess of St Brigid's foundation at Kildare, who is noted in the Pictish king list as having come to the founding of St Brigid's church at Abernethy in southern Pictland, in the time of king Nectan macMorbet, around the end of the sixth century. In the role of the abbots lay an important difference betweeen the Celtic Churches and the Church as ruled from Rome. In the Roman scheme of things, the bishop was of prime importance; in the Celtic Churches, the bishop had no territorial authority, no authority to impose doctrine, and very little judicial or disciplinary power. His role was a sacramental one. Bishops were greatly respected, but strictly as holy men. Power lay with the abbots.

The Irish Church remained a federation rather than a hierarchy on the Roman model. In exile, the Anglian prince Oswald, son of Aethelfrith, had lived on Iona. When he became king of Northumbria in 633, he sent to the island for a bishop to come and teach Christianity to the pagan Angles. The Northumbrian Church, from its first base on Lindisfarne, was established on the Celtic model by its first bishop, St Aidan, sent from Iona. But, by the middle of the seventh century, it had shaken off its Celtic aspects and conformed to the rule and doctrines of Rome, as expounded by the papally appointed incumbents of the recently established bishopric of Canterbury. Northumbria's up-and-coming clerics, like Wilfred, were, by then, Anglians, not Scots. At the Synod of Whitby in 664, called by king Oswiu of Northumbria, Wilfred won the debate with the Ionan bishop Colman over the central issues of the dating of Easter and the form of a monk's tonsure. In a secular age, these seem minor matters, but the Celtic churchmen, with a long tradition not merely of independence, but of maintaining the faith when it had all but collapsed elsewhere, saw the abandonment of these practices as a rejection of 200 years of devoted labour. It was a further source of gall that the changes were being promoted by their erstwhile daughter church in Northumbria. A vital aspect of the society both of Scots and Picts, inseparable from the mores of a warrior-led aristocracy, was a passion for prestige. The precept of Christian humility notwithstanding, the priests also shared this thin-skinned prickly sense of pride and honour. Bede relates that the first bishop of Canterbury, pope Gregory's emissary, St Augustine, offended clerics from the Churches already established in Britain when he refused to rise from his chair to greet them on their arrival at a meeting. Such things were far from being considered trivial, and Wilfred's clever sneer, borrowed from the headquarters briefing of a Lateran missive was both insulting and wounding:

> 'The only people who are stupid enough to disagree with the whole world are these Scots and their obstinate adherents the Picts and the Britons, who inhabit only a portion of these two islands in the remote ocean.' (Bede, iii, 25)

(He appears, incidentally, to have been the first person to identify and patronise what was much later called 'the Celtic fringe'.) It was a bitter pill for the monks of Iona to admit to their own people that they, and the great Columba before them, had been practising a flawed rite. Even though their abbot, Adamnan, who died in 704, accepted the Roman view, his own community continued to reject it at least until 716.

CHAPTER TEN

Origins

If it seems a little strange to discuss the island peoples' views of their own origins in Chapter Ten rather than earlier, there is a simple explanation. All the written information that exists on the subject comes from the time when they had already accepted the doctrines of Christianity, and it was written by scribes who, if not monks themselves, had at least had a Christian education at a monastery school. These writers undoubtedly had at their disposal a great deal of information, passed on orally, maintained in customs and ceremonies, or perhaps written in texts that have long been lost, passed on from previous generations. Many precious or significant objects and articles were preserved, each with its own story: relics and reliquaries of pioneer saints, miraculous pebbles, ornamented book boxes, standing stones. The most plentiful source of ancient information was the Irish tradition, which was also carried to Scotland by the incoming Gaels. There is less material from the ancient Britons, but enough to establish some of their tradition. With the exception of their stone-carvings and a few linguistic hints, what we know of the Picts comes from the comments of others, first Romans, then Gaels and Britons, all with their own perspective on the northerners. The Anglo-Saxons, once firmly established, recorded observations on their Celtic neighbours; Bede's Latin *Ecclesiastical History of the English People*, written on Tyneside in 731, is an important source.

None of these documents are 'history', in the sense of being an objective record of actions and events. Even Bede, who was far ahead of his time in this respect, was writing to sustain and advance the English Church established by St Augustine and only recently put on a national basis by Theodore of Tarsus. Partisans deeply engaged in the political and moral debates of their own times, the Irish and British had little concept of objective historical accounts, as we understand the notion. History had to be shaped to underwrite the present and the hoped-for future, a process that is clearly revealed in the Irish people's and the Scots' own account of their origins. They preserved the traditional knowledge, or myth, that they had come, as a people, to Ireland from somewhere else. What the Picts believed of their own origins has been lost, as has what the Britons of Strathclyde thought of theirs. (The Scots, for their own reasons, produced a theory on the Picts' origins, which the Britons also picked up on.)

Thus the Irish people's account of their own beginnings, as we have it, is not an 'original' one. It has been heavily influenced by the need to adapt their traditional story, as they had preserved it up to the sixth century, to the demands of Christianity, once they had been converted to the new religion. In essence, it is a genealogy, with some biographical and geographical details added. Like other such legends of early peoples, it traces the descent of the whole people, as a single kinship group, from a single ancestor of high prestige. In pagan times, this ancestor would have been a god (in the preserved Gaelic myths of the *Ulster Cycle* and others, there is still plenty of evidence of pseudohistorical kings and heroes fathered by Celtic gods such as Lugh, Dagdá, and Donn). With the adoption of Christianity, a heathen pedigree was no longer acceptable, and a satisfactory alternative had to be found. The learned men found their model in the Bible narrative of the Old Testament, which itself is, among other things, a genealogical document of the Hebrew kings. If this was not the actual inspiration for the genealogies of Irish and Scottish kings, it certainly influenced them. The source was not so much the Bible, of which St Jerome's Latin version, the Vulgate, had been completed in the late fourth century, as various commentators on the Scriptural texts, such as the third-century Christian chronicler, Eusebius, and his successors, Orosius in the sixth century and Isidore of Seville in the seventh. Eusebius, a Palestinian bishop, whose *Chronicon* set out to synchronise events in Christian and pagan history, was especially influential on the way in which the various forms of the Annals were set out.

The earliest Old Irish texts do not survive, but many were still available in the twelfth century, when a collection of ancient Irish documents by various writers from different periods was put together in the *Lebor Gabála Érenn*, 'Book of the Taking of Ireland'. The scheme of the book is based on six successive invasions of, or arrivals in, Ireland.

The first is that of Cesair, grand-daughter of Noah, sent to Ireland to escape the Flood. She is accompanied by her father, three other men, and 50 women. Their aim is to procreate and populate the land. Three hundred and twelve years later Partholón, also of Biblical stock, arrives. He and his people, the Partholonians, are descended from Magog. They settle in the east, but are ravaged by a plague. After a gap of 30 years come Nemed and the Nemedians, from the region of the Caspian Sea. They settle more successfully than their predecessors, but they encounter a ferocious seaborne people called the Fomorians, noted as coming from the lands to the north of Ireland. The Fomorians establish their own colonies, doing battle with the Partholonians and the Nemedians. The fourth invasion is that of the Fir Bolg, the first people in the book to have a Celtic name ('men of Builg': a name often suggested as being cognate with that of the continental Celtic tribe of the Belgae), and said to have come many generations after the Nemedians. They are represented as short in stature and dark-haired.

Thirty-seven years after them come the magic-endowed *Tuatha dé Danann*, 'people of the god Danann', a name that is still not satisfactorily explained. The Tuatha dé Danann defeat the Fir Bolg and the Fomorians and institute the era in which much of early Irish myth and legend is set. The final invasion, 297 years later, is that of the sons of Míl Espáine, literally 'soldier of Spain', and his eponymous followers the Milesians. Despite his name, Míl's career begins in the east, in Scythia, as a military leader. Later, in Egypt, he commands the armies of the pharaoh Nectanebo. He marries Scota, daughter of the pharaoh, and she bears him four sons, among them Eber Finn and Eremón. In fulfilment of a druidic prophecy, they leave Egypt for the unknown island of Ireland, but stop off in Spain, the land of his birth. There he dies and Scota (whose name can mean 'Ireland' or 'Irishwoman') carries on to Ireland. Míl himself is taken as the direct ancestor of the Irish-Scottish Gaels, and their kings' genealogies stem from him. Éremon was the son of Scota and Míl who ruled the northern half of Ireland, and to him the kings of Scots traced their own descent. A feature of their investitures was the recital of their pedigree back through Éremon and Míl to 'Eber the first Scot', grandson of Goídel Glas (see page 127), who was himself son of an earlier Scota. A genealogy of William I, king of Scots, from 1185, has been preserved, which does not stop even at Eber, but goes back another 23 generations before him, all the way to Noah. Eber Finn ruled the southern half of Ireland, until rivalry between the brothers brought about his death at Eremón's hands. From this Milesian conquest stems the Gaelic language.

It was, for a long time, assumed that, at the basis of this ancient legend, or conflation of legends, lay the real fact of a migration or migrations from a far-off eastern homeland to the new home in the furthest west. With the general abandonment by archaeologists of the idea of successive invasions, this assumption has, in recent years, seemed increasingly uncertain. How, then, did the story of the invasions arise? The compilers of the *Lebor Gabála*, as has been noted, were heavily influenced by the Bible ('theorists and mythographers' Henri Hubert called them). There are strong echoes in their book of the story of the wanderings of the Israelites: their Egyptian sojourn, their wars, and their final establishment in a promised land. In addition, so as to be able to establish a Biblical pedigree for Irish, and later Scottish, kings, it was essential to establish a link with the Israelites and with the part of the world they were known to inhabit. Coupled with the knowledge that such learned and semimagical techniques as iron-smelting and smithying had been passed on from an eastern source, it is possible, at least, to frame the outline of the way in which the migration story evolved.

The *Lebor Gabála* has been described as 'a laborious attempt to combine parts of the native teaching with Hebrew mythology embellished with medieval legend.' (MacKillop) The bald outline is greatly elaborated and complicated with sometimes contradictory or anachronistic events. Elements from it are found in many other sources, often with differences of detail. The task, then, is to try to identify the real events which underlie the invasion stories. As Henri Hubert commented:

> 'They [the authors] did not invent the Fomorians or the Fir Bolg or the Tuatha Dé Danann. Most of the episodes revolve around the great seasonal feasts of the Irish year. They are myths . . . but among these myths there are traditions of a historical kind, and names which belong to history.'

Historians have discounted the first two 'invasions' of the *Lebor Gabála* as being too obviously concocted back-projections by later writers. But the Nemedians are thought to have traces of historical truth mingled in the highly coloured account of their battles with the Fomorians. And the latter, when stripped of mythological traits and despite some anachronistic colouring by later scribes who knew the marauding Vikings, have been plausibly seen as inhabitants of the Western Isles, which show many signs of prehistoric habitation. Professor T. F. O'Rahilly identified the Nemedians with a prehistoric people he called the Érainn, speakers of a conjectured *p*-Celtic language. In the *Lebor Gabála*, the Nemedians are seen as the ancestors of the (Irish) *Cruithne* and of the *Bretnaigh Cluada*, 'Britons of Clyde'. The tentative linking of the Fir Bolg with the Belgae need not imply a heavy traffic between the dunes of Flanders and the sandy bays of southern Ireland; it is easy to suppose a congruence, but Irish *bolg* has meanings that could be relevant: 'bay' for example. Other possibly related tribal names are found separated by wide stretches of territory, as we saw with the Damnonii in southern Scotland, and Dumnonii in southwest England.

The semidivine Tuatha Dé Danann are harder to relate to any set of real people; they represent rather an idealised era which ends fittingly, in one tale anyway, when on their defeat by the Milesians they retire to Tir na nOg, the mythical land of the ever-young. In other versions, they retreat underground, in the many barrows and raths of the Irish landscape, and their race becomes that of the *Sídh*, or fairy folk. The Milesians are the first overtly Gaelic-speaking people to be mentioned. Part of their story indeed is the creation of the Gaelic speech, appropriately after the Biblical Tower of Babel episode, by Goídel Glas, on the instructions of his grandfather, Fénius Farsaid. Goídel Glas, his name later found as Gathelus, was son of Niúl, and – like the later Míl Espáine – his mother was Scota, a pharaoh's daughter. In one of the clever inserted links that help to give the story plausibility, Goídel's by-name of *Glas*, 'green', refers to a mark left by a snakebite. He was cured of this in Egypt by Moses, who also prophesied that his descendants would one day live in a country where no snakes were to be found. And, sure enough, Ireland is well known for its lack of snakes . . .

Also found at a later stage in the Milesian story, after they have reached Ireland, is their encounter with three goddesses, each of whom asks the Milesians to name the land after her: Banba, Ériu, and Fódla. These names are closely identified with the land of the Gaels. Ériu is preserved in Erin, and also, according to some toponymists, in Earn and Strathearn – seen as names brought by Scottish colonists into Pictish territory. Banba has (more dubiously) been seen in the name Banff, while Fódla is seen in the name Atholl, as 'ford of Fódla'. Not the least interesting aspect of the Milesian story is the implication that the speakers of Gaelic came to an Ireland that was Celtic-speaking, but of a *p*-Celtic language. In the words of professor James MacKillop, referring to political power:

'Milesian hegemony spread to all corners of Ireland.' (*Dictionary of Celtic Mythology*)

From a modest start in the sixth century, the descendants of Goídel Glas and Míl would achieve the same result in Scotland.

Impressive and suggestive as the ancient Irish legends are – one of the oldest literatures of Europe – there are few reliable facts that can be extracted from them. Only archaeology can establish definite knowledge of the prehistoric period. The basic forms of the legendary history can then be compared with the modern explanation arrived at by the accrued work of historians, antiquarians, linguists, and latterly archaeologists, between the 14th century and the 21st century. Needless to say, this process has not been a smoothly progressing one; it has been marked by storms of controversy and prejudice, much of it on the Scottish side documented in William Ferguson's *The Identity of the Scottish Nation*.

The Scots, of course, were relative newcomers to Scotland compared with the Picts and the Britons. In Ireland, their roots went back as far as memory and imagination could stretch; as colonists in Pictland, they were upstarts. Awareness of this is likely to have coloured their own versions of history, including the history of other peoples. Bede, writing more than 200 years after the arrival of the Dàl Riata, relates a story

about the origin of the Picts that he has clearly picked up from
the Scots:

' . . . it is said some Picts from Scythia put to sea in a few
longships, and were driven by storms around the coasts of
Britain, arriving at length on the north coast of Ireland.
Here they found the nation of the Scots, from whom they
asked permission to settle, but their request was refused . . .
The Scots replied that there was not room for them both,
but said: "We can give you good advice. There is another
island not far to the east, which we often see in the distance
on clear days. Go and settle there if you wish; should you
meet resistance, we will come to your help." So the Picts
crossed into Britain, and began to settle in the north of the
island, since the Britons were in possession of the south.
Having no women with them, these Picts asked wives of
the Scots, who consented on condition that, when any dispute arose, they should choose a king from the female royal
line rather than the male . . . This tradition continues among
the Picts to this day.' (Bede, I, i)

This famous tale is found in a number of different versions in
old Irish writings. It has two fireworks figuratively attached to
it: the suggestion that the Picts owe their habitat and their continuing existence as a people to the Scots, and the implication
that they, in the case of 'disputes', chose their kings on the
basis of descent from the mother, and not, as with the Scots
themselves and every other recorded society in Western Europe, from the father. The 15th-century *Book of Lecain* specifically links these points to the assertion that:

' . . . of the men of Erin has been the chieftainship over
Cruthentuath (Pictland) from that time ever since.'

The Britons added their own twist by fostering a version of
the story that states that the Picts first came to them, as a rov-
ing Scythian war band that fought and was defeated by them,

before asking for wives. But 'the Britons would not marry their daughters to foreigners of another country without knowing of what race they were, and aliens they were, moreover, and they refused their petition, and after their refusal they went to Ireland, and married women of the Gael.' (W. F. Skene, *Chronicles of the Picts and Scots*) This version neatly established the Britons at the top of the 'We were here first' debate – not just a prestige point but a significant position in matters such as land and boundary disputes.

'Scythian', incidentally, was a generic term as ethnically and geographically indistinct as Celtic; it referred to the inhabitants of a vast swathe of northern Europe from the Black Sea to the Norwegian fiords, and its use does not shed much light on the origins of the Picts. It is of some interest, in that it suggests a northern origin for them. The Gaelic name for Pict is *Cruithne*, which, in *qu*-Celtic form, is cognate with the Old Welsh *Priteni*. Both terms originally meant an inhabitant of Britain, and not specifically a Pict. The Gaels knew of Cruithne before any of them set sail across the North Channel. Sharing the north Ulster coastland with the Gaelic-speaking Dàl Riata was a people known as being of the race of Cruithne, whose tribal name by the sixth century CE was the Dàl Araidhe. Although regarded as a subject people by the Ulster Gaels, the Dàl Araidhe sometimes succeeded in possessing the overkingship of the province. There was also a group known as the Cruithin, established in Meath, in the very centre of Ireland. These are generally supposed to be the same people as the Caledonian Picts, and to have entered Ireland at an unknown time from north Britain. Possibly, though, the movement was in the other direction. There is a lingering account, found in several different ancient sources, that the Picts came into north Britain from the north, settling first in Orkney and spreading south from there. This does not fit badly with the notion of a departure from the northern coast of Ireland, via the Western Isles. Intriguing as these matters are, they have been shelved or ignored by historians for lack of convincing evidence to support any particular theory. Even the language of the Dàl Araidhe has a question mark over it. Was it Pictish? Or Brittonic? Had it been Pictish and been supplanted by Gaelic? What were the relations between those Irish-located Cruithne and their Pictish neighbours across the narrow sea, the nearest being the Epidii of Kintyre, identified by Ptolemy in 150CE, but unheard of since?

No Pictish list of their kings survives; indeed, no Pictish document of any kind has been traced. Two separate groups of lists survive, known as the 'Pictish Chronicle', and written down as copies long after the Pictish period. Both groups have several variant manuscript versions. The first Pictish king of whom we have knowledge, other than from these lists, is Bridei, son of Maelcon, who reigned around 558–83. However, some 30 kings are noted as preceding him. While some of these, in the sixth and fifth centuries, are allowed some basis of historical existence, the majority are regarded as fictitious or legendary. Marjorie Anderson ascribes the early kings listed in both groups to a common source, written down 'not much after 724. It had very possibly been begun a good deal earlier'. After 724, the lists diverge. One group, known as the 'P' list, uses Pictish names (though somewhat Gaelicised by the later scribes) and conforms well with the dates given in the Annals. The making of the 'P' list is associated with the monastery at Abernethy. The other list, referred to as the 'Q' list by Mrs Anderson, apparently fell into abeyance for 60 years or so after 724, then was resuscitated, with a number of errors in the 'gap' years, though, from 780 onwards, it is quite reliable, if more heavily Gaelicised than the 'P' list. The 'Q' list is linked with St Andrews and the records kept by its bishopric after the tenth century. Both lists begin with Cruithne, whose name simply means 'Pict', and the 'P' list follows him with the names of his seven sons, which correspond to the provinces of Pictland.

Although no Pictish tale of origins is preserved, we do have, from a tenth-century Scottish document, the so-called 'Pictish Chronicle'. This combines a brief account (taken from Isidore of Seville, a great rehasher of legendary information) of the 'history of the ancient Picts', together with a sequence of Pictish kings and their reign lengths, and occasional brief items of information relating to a particular king or reign. The earlier kings, and especially those earlier than Nectan Morbet, who is credited with the foundation of the priory at Abernethy, are regarded as being increasingly fictional, though their names have provided a ready source of speculation for anyone trying to find bottom in the dark pool of Pictish mythology and history. Most scholars would, however, agree with Euan MacKie that:

> 'The archaeological evidence, though sparse . . . is increasingly suggesting that the majority of the Picts were descended from the Iron Age, or even the Late Bronze Age tribes of the same area.'

The oldest traditions of Welsh speakers are preserved in a collection, its full title, *Pedair Cainc y Mabinogi*, 'The Four Branches of the *Mabinogi*' (which may mean 'tale of youth'). The branches are the tales of *Pwll*, *Branwen*, *Manawydan*, and *Math*; although the surviving manuscript sources are no earlier than the 14th century, the tales clearly belong to a much older period. First collated in the twelfth century, their origins go far back in the oral tradition, linking the stories of mortals to those of divine or semidivine beings, as in the Irish legends. *Pwll* deals with the exploits of a ruler of Dyfed, who travels to the Otherworld, marries Rhiannon, and is father of Pryderi. *Branwen* tells the story of the offspring of the sea god Llyr, and brings Ireland into the action, recounting how the giant ruler of Britain, Bendigeidfran (Bran), whose seat is at Harlech, gives his sister Branwen in marriage to the Irish king Matholwch, but invades Ireland when Matholwch treats

Branwen dishonourably. *Manawydan* recounts how the brother of Bendigeidfran retrieves Rhiannon (whom he has married after Pwll's death), and Pryderi from a magical spell. *Math* is the son of Mathonwy, an accomplished magician, who rules Gwynedd. The story that bears his name is a complicated but highly exciting tale of heroism, love, adultery, and vengeance. Among its characters are Gwydion, the magician; his sister, Arianrhod, 'Silver Disc' (perhaps a moon goddess of earlier time), mother of the twins, Dylan and Lleu Law Gyffes, 'fair one of the steady hand'; and Blodeuedd, the beautiful woman made from flowers who forsakes Lleu for the hunter Gronw Pebyr.

The most authoritative manuscript form is in the *Red Book of Hergest*, compiled between c.1382 and 1410, largely by the scribe Hywel Fychan fab Howel Goch o Fuellt. It also contains other ancient texts. The *Mabinogi* stories, plus others, are also recorded in the *White Book of Rhydderch*, written down around 1325, probably at a site in the southwestern kingdom of Deheubarth. Fragments are also found in other 15th-century manuscripts. The first English version was Lady Charlotte Guest's *Mabinogion* of 1838–49, which also included other legends from the *Red Book of Hergest*, including *Culhwch ac Olwen*, *Breuddwyd Rhonabwy* ('The Dream of Rhonabwy'), *Breuddwyd Macsen Wledig* ('The Dream of Magnus Maximus'), and other tales that combine historical and mythical characters.

The differences between the Welsh and the Irish legends are striking, and should give pause to anyone looking for a common 'Celtic' culture in late prehistoric or early historic times. How far the Welsh legends embrace an older wider Brittonic-speaking region is hard to say. The geographical spread of the *Mabinogi* is the Irish Sea region. But the Gododdin story was preserved until written in the surviving *Book of Aneirin* from the 13th century, just as the memory of the *Gwyr y Gogledd*, 'Men of the North', was preserved. 'Welsh', of course, was a name coined by the Anglo-Saxons, and the Ancient Britons who survived in Wales referred to themselves as *Y Gwir Frythoniaid*, 'the true Britons', and as *Cymry*, or compatriots, from the Brittonic *combrogos*.

The earliest record of Welsh history is the Latin work known as the *Historia Brittonum*, 'History of the Britons', compiled in the ninth century. The name of Nennius (*Niniaw*) has been associated for more than a millennium with this text. Modern scholars regard him not as its author – if it had a single author – but as a kind of editor, copying, collating, and rewriting more ancient works. Nennius lived at a time when classical learning was in decline; his Latin is much less assured, if also less ornate, than Gildas's in the sixth century (see Chapter Eleven). The work's main aim was to set out a history of the British struggle against the Anglo-Saxons, including references to a north British campaign similar to that described in the 'Gododdin' poem, and among the resources used were a life of St Germanus, a list of the 'cities' of Britain, and copies of the royal genealogies of six Anglo-Saxon kingdoms, as well as the chronicles of Latin writers, including Jerome, and Isidore of Seville. The *Historia* is one of the earliest works to refer to Arthur (see Chapter Twelve). It is the source of the story of Cunedda and the tribal migration he led – or may have led – to North Wales. But it has nothing to say of earlier events. The Welsh kings seem to have been content to trace their pedigrees back to the time of Roman domination: Magnus Maximus plays a founding part in some of their pedigrees.

CHAPTER ELEVEN

International Relations, Kings, and Laws

Contacts between Celtic societies were well established from ancient times. Exploration by archaeologists of the rich continental Celtic burial sites whose artefacts are characterised as being in the La Tène and, earlier, the Hallstatt, styles, has made it clear that for the Celtic peoples, trading and diplomacy with groupings of other peoples was a regular procedure. The chieftaincies of the Hallstatt culture and the warrior aristocracies of the La Tène period both grew rich by occupying pivotal points on north-south communication routes in middle Europe. They held the line between the producers of the north and the consumers of the Mediterranean coastlands, not as brigands but as maintainers of an established and profitable transit operation. Inevitably, they became transmission points of ideas, of linguistic trends, of new customs, as well as of raw materials and manufactured articles. In a new opening chapter to Dr Nora Chadwick's *The Celts* (1997), professor Barry Cunliffe notes how Greek influence from ports like Massilia (Marseilles) spread up the Rhône and Saône river valleys in the fifth century BCE:

'To the élites of west central Europe, Mediterranean luxury goods were symbols of their privileged status. By carefully controlling the inflow of these exotics, they were able to display the signs of their power for all to see.'

Contacts, influences, and exchanges of this kind go back to the early Bronze Age and, in a simpler form, to even earlier.

The tribes who lived north of Hadrian's Wall and in Ireland were not outside this system, though they represented the end of the trading-line. rather than a junction or toll point. In the Roman period, their southward forays each time a Roman governor was replaced show that they were informed of what was happening within the Roman province. The famous 'coordinated' attack by Picts, Scots, and Attacotti in 367 suggests that there were means of arranging for joint action and for making it effective. Such operations require a good deal of liaison. The organisation of trade and the exchange of goods can be relatively easily understood, especially if the role of middlemen is granted. In the prehistoric period, no relationship between the persons at either end of a long trade-exchange line need be assumed, or even between others on the line, except for those who were adjacent or near to one another. Later, the existence of long-range links and personal travel is clear. There is evidence in gravestone inscriptions of Greek and Syrian traders operating as far north as Hadrian's Wall during the Roman occupancy. Wherever there were numbers of troops on a regular payroll, the traders would follow, no matter how remote and exotic the location.

The nature and methods of diplomatic contact between peoples are much less apparent. In the cadre of professionals within the tribes, 'diplomats' are not included as a group. Such roles were encompassed by people classified in other ways, but presumably drawn from the ranks of the druids (later priests) and the bards and historians. Men in these roles were members of leading families and possessed the necessary prestige, education, and authority. The freedom of passage granted to members of these orders may have been recognition as much of their diplomatic work as of their artistic status and abilities. Mastering of other languages was an essential part of this work, since communication was oral (language-learning might in some cases have been a useful by-product of fostering or hostage-taking, at least when the hostage survived). The achievement of treaties and agreements might be recorded in various ways, as by the exchange of symbolic objects and gifts, and perhaps the erection of standing stones, but the details do not seem to have been written down. Although he should be considered a special case, we see Columcille acting in this sort of capacity at the 'Synod' of Drum Ceatt, in 575, where difficult negotiations between the two Dàl Riadas and between Dàl Riada and Ulster had to be carried on. He is likely to have been a prime mover in setting up this event, rather than a delegate of one side or another. Emissaries and adjudicators were necessary to deal with other intertribal matters, such as royal marriages, the giving of hostages, the ransoming of prisoners, and the exchange of gifts. Arranging the details of military cooperation and coordination would seem to require a different set of skills, but the same high level of communication abilities.

Perhaps in matters such as this, the regular practice of seeking to make royal marriage arrangements beyond the tribe again has a part to play. Relations between cousin- or even brother-kings were by no means necessarily always friendly but, when they were amicable, the family link must have eased the potential difficulties of cooperation, by providing an umbrella of joint royal patronage under which mutually suspicious subchiefs could meet and discuss the mechanics of alliance and of joint attack or defence.

The missionary aspect of Christianity brought its own kind of contact between peoples. Following the efforts of the Briton, St Patrick (thought to have come from a prominent family in the Romano-British city of Carlisle), his predecessors and his successors (he died around 461), many of the Irish tribal kingdoms had adopted Christianity. The Dàl Riadan colonists were already Christians and, from early in the sixth century, determined missions to convert the Picts to Christianity were under way. The custodians of the bardic and druidic traditions had come to terms with the new religion and, to a degree,

Christianity had absorbed parts of the old tradition. It is not clear how far the first Hebridean monasteries were mission stations and how far they were simply religious communities founded in 'desert' places, where the monks could pursue their austere avocations in peace. But a strong teaching and missionary purpose was evident from the fifth century at least, and considerable progress had been made. The king of Strathclyde, Rhydderch, who died in 570, was a Christian. The Picts, it seems, were then still pagan, yet, even in his lifetime, St Patrick had written of 'apostate Picts' who bought Christians as slaves (*Letter to Coroticus*). Coroticus (Ceredig) was a British king who ruled at Dumbarton and had Irish Christians among his slaves. This suggests that some, at least, had accepted Christianity and then reverted back to paganism. Who or where these apostate Picts were is not known. But it seems likely that fifth-century missionaries from Whithorn took their message into Pictish territory, and established churches in some places in the name of their own founder, Ninian. These isolated churches may not have survived, and required refounding in the course of the Christian expansion of the sixth and seventh centuries. It is notable that a string of churches dedicated to St Ninian follows the eastern coastline all the way up to Shetland, a long way from Whithorn. Ninian had no connection with Iona, and a missionary venture originating from Iona would not have had any reason to use his name. Despite the hostile rivalry between the druid Broichan and Columcille, described by Adamnan in his *Life of St Columba*, the Picts appear to have been relatively tolerant in religious matters; although St Columba did not convert king Bridei to Christianity, he was allowed to preach and to send evangelising monks into Pictland. The inference is that individuals could adopt Christianity, even though the official cult was still that of the druids. But, once the king was converted, Christianity became the 'state' religion.

In 540, the British ecclesiastic, Gildas, wrote a text, *De Excidio Britanniae*, 'The Destruction of Britain', intended not as a history or description, but as a moral tract for those in charge of his own society, including Maelgwyn or Maelcon, king of Gwynedd, and possible father of the Pictish king, Bridei. Some choice uncomplimentary epithets are reserved for Maelgwyn; Gildas was no respecter of persons. He also makes vituperative reference to the Picts and Scots as ' . . . foul hordes . . . like dark throngs of worms who wriggle out of narrow fissures in the rock when the sun is high and the weather grows warm.'

Because he is specially singled out for criticism by Gildas, we know more about this sixth-century figure than about most early regional kings. Also known as *Maelgwyn Hir*, 'Longfellow', he was clearly taller than the average. He had a distinguished father in Cadwallon, who conquered the Irish who had settled in north Wales. Although he ruled Anglesey, his main strong-hold seems to have been Degannwy. Gildas describes him as generous in charitable giving, as well as profuse in sin, and he is also mentioned in a number of biographies of saints, for both these reasons. One of Maelgwyn's misdeeds was to maintain a troop of bards at his court. While they, no doubt, sang the king's praises, the bards, at this time and later, also preserved a great deal of verse from pre-Christian times, which earned them the enmity of the evangelists. It seems that Maelgwyn had a taste for older traditions. He had strong connections with the Cumbric peoples of the north, and legend also links him with the bard, Taliesin, in a contest in which Taliesin releases his master, Elphin, held in prison at Maelgwyn's orders. Maelgwyn died of 'the yellow plague', in or around the year 547.

The author of *The Destruction of Britain* was one of the *Gwyr y Gogledd*, Men of the North. According to a biographer who lived some centuries later, he was born in *Arecluta*, the lower Clyde area, around 500CE. He was well educated, both in Christian doctrine and in Latin rhetoric and literature; the same biographical source says he was taught by St Illtud, who kept a school for promising and well-born boys. Gildas became a monk and, from the evidence of his own work, he clearly was an impassioned believer in the virtues of Celtic monasticism. The historical information in his work is incidental, and used only to point his moral. Writing in the time of relative peace that followed the British victory of Mount Badon, his is a prophetic warning, that sinfulness will result in a further catalogue of downfall and calamity.

Apart from its historical importance, though many historians have cursed him for what he might have put in but did not, Gildas's 'Letter' as he refers to it, is interesting, as it seems to be a purely individual effort. He was not a bishop or abbot and had no formal position of power. A burning desire to say what he had to say seems to have driven him on. He is the last spokesman – in polished Latin – of the Romano-British world, disappearing fast in his day. The pagan Anglo-Saxons, the barbarian Picts and Scots, are equally scorned. He harks back with sad pride to the exploits of Ambrosius (*Emrys Wledig*). There can be no doubt that Gildas pursued his theme in sermons and other letters and writings, which have not been preserved. Although he was, unsurprisingly, an unwelcome figure in Wales, his influence in other parts of the 'Celtic fringe' appears to have been strong, notably in Ireland and in Brittany, where he died, around 565.

Much of his account is backward-looking but it clearly implies that relations between the kingdoms were not good. Strathclyde and the other British kingdoms to its south had a bitter struggle on their hands against the Angles of both Bernicia and its neighbouring kingdom of Deira, in what is now central and eastern Yorkshire, and their efforts to drive the newcomers back into the sea were a failure. Inexorably, the Angles pushed their frontiers out into British territory. Aethelfrith, king of Bernicia from 593, became king also of Deira and united the two territories in the large and expansion-minded kingdom of Northumbria. He was master of all the land between Humber and Tweed. The rise of Northumbria intensified the Britons' efforts to hold their own territories. The poem, 'Y Gododdin', ascribed to the Cumbric-speaking sixth-century bard, Aneirin, tells of a heroic but disastrous assault on Catraeth (taken to be Catterick), in Deira, by a band of 300 warriors, mostly of the Gododdin (Votadini) tribe, sent by their king Mynyddog Mwynfawr, 'the wealthy', from his fortress in Lothian, which may have been sited on what later became the Castle Rock of Edinburgh:

> 'From men who had been mead-nourished and wine-nourished
> A bright array charged forth, who had drunk together from the bowl.
> For the feast in the mountain stronghold they were to perish—
> Too many I have lost of my true kinsmen.
> Of the three hundred gold-torqued men who attacked Catraeth,
> Alas! Only one escaped.'

These elegiac verses, dating from the mid-sixth century, have been jokingly described by Kenneth Jackson as 'the first Scottish poem'. At the time, of course, Lothian was not part of Scotland, which did not then exist. John T. Koch in an article, 'The Place of "Y Gododdin" in the History of Scotland', notes that the leader of the band is named as 'son of Golistan' – the English name Wulfstan – and concludes that these Celtic warriors, attacking an Anglian fortress, were in fact led by an Angle or Anglo-Saxon. Wulfstan, in his view, was an example of 'brittonicised pagan Anglian generalissimos'; the text itself does not shed any light on his motives, though it does describe a forthright character:

> 'It was usual for Wolstan's son – though his father was no sovereign lord – that what he say be heeded.'

Picts are also mentioned as forming part of the host. Dr Kathleen Hughes notes the presence of 'the foreign horseman, the young only son of Cian from beyond Bannog'.

Bannog was the name for the hills between Stirling and Dumbarton, still preserved in the name Bannockburn. She suggested that that three others named may also be Picts. Rather than being a purely Gododdin group, it seems that the war party included a number of freebooting warriors, who had joined either through obligation of some kind or, perhaps, at invitation. Koch warns against reading too much into such presences: 'In trying to glean these dark-age political realities from diverse and fragmentary evidence, it is easy to be deceived by our strongly-developed present-day national and ethnolinguistic senses of group identity.' In other words, we cannot re-create, from the available material, the loyalties and motives of these fighters. We should also remember that, even in an era when an army might consist only of 2000 or 3000 men, the Gododdin band was a notably small one: a picked set of champions, rather than a full military force. It may be that, as some writers have suggested, the 300 fighters each brought retainers, not mentioned by the poet. But it seems improbable that their deaths, at least, would not be mentioned. The very preservation of this poem, when other detail is so scanty, can make the event seem more significant than perhaps it was. Nevertheless, defeat was more frequent than victory for the Britons in the prolonged struggle. The kings of the Picts and Scots appear to have remained largely aloof from this conflict. If the British kings asked them for help, it was not forthcoming.

Partly by analogy with the better-recorded Irish pattern from which they emerged, and partly through such Scottish records as the *Senchus fer nAlban*, 'Tradition of the Men of Alba', a document from the tenth century, but using information compiled in the late seventh century, the organisation of the Scots is much better known than that of the Britons or Picts. They were a homogeneous group; there never appears to been any suggestion that they 'absorbed' Picts previously living in the territory. But still we hear nothing of the Epidii, the tribe noted by Ptolemy as occupying Kintyre in the second century, and whose name implies *p*-Celtic language speakers. Though nothing is known of them or their fate, it has been noted that 'horse' names were prominent there in Gaelic times, as in MacEachern, 'son of the horse lord'. There is surely a suggestion here of absorption of communities, the question being which absorbed which? Evidently the Epidii either adopted Gaelic or their traditions, if nothing more, were passed on to the Scots.

The Scots who colonised Argyll and the inner isles divided into three main tribal groups: the Cineal Gabhrain, the Cineal Loairn, and the Cineal Aonghus, with each occupying a distinct district. From the Cineal Gabhrain also emerged the Cineal Comghall of Cowal. Each of these *cinele* had a chief, or king (Gaelic *righ*). One of these kings was also the overking of the Dàl Riata. For many years, the size and prestige of the Cineal Gabhrain meant that its king was the overking. Below the kings, in each *cineal*, were further area chiefs, at the head of island or mainland communities, and below them were the heads of individual families within the kin group. Each of these leaders had his share of authority within his domain, and each owed loyalty to his next chief and the king. All shared a history, religious beliefs, a language, and a range of social customs and traditions. To the overking were due certain duties and payments of tribute from all the subkingdoms. The duties included military service both by land and sea, with each household assessed for its contribution. The *Senchus fer nAlban* shows that a king who mustered the forces of Dàl Riada had a precise idea of how many households his subkings controlled, and the number of fighting men they should provide. It was not a haphazard business. One can picture his captain counting them off at the muster, rank by rank and boat by boat.

Kings were made, not born, albeit from a narrow section of society. This was the *derbfine*, or kindred group, consisting of all the men who could claim descent up to the third generation from a king – a range of brothers, cousins, uncles, and nephews, whose numbers could rise into double figures if a king were long-lived. The competition among them could, and often did, make for strife within the *cineal*. In the case of the choice of an overking, the *derbfine* of the incumbent would provide the candidates. But here, the choice might be challenged or repudiated by another of the *cinele*, either for personal reasons of opposition or because it sought to install its own man. The long tenure of the overkingship by the Cineal Gabhrain seems to have been increasingly resented by the other main kindred groups of the Dàl Riata. Relations between these groups were often hostile and frequently broke out in open warfare. The Cineal Loairn, squeezed between its own kindred to the south and Pictish territory to the north, was often restive. It may have been its efforts to expand northwards that brought Bridei's Picts down on the Scots in 550. The foot-shaped indentation in the stone surface of Dunadd is often taken as the mark of a place where kings were inaugurated. Setting the new king's foot here was assumed to be part of the ceremony. This is quite likely but, although Dunadd was plainly an important fort, there is no evidence to prove that it was the royal centre of Dàl Riada: it may have been the headquarters of a subking.

After Kenneth MacAlpin, the kings of Scots were inaugurated on the moot hill of Scone, which may have been used for the same purpose by the Pictish kings of Fortriu. Though events like the crowning of Alexander III, in the open air outside Scone Abbey in 1249, may well have been modelled on well-known and long-established precedents, we do not have any details. But it seems likely that, until the ninth century, the Stone of Destiny, brought across from Ireland as a sacred possession of the Dàl Riata, was kept at Dunstaffnage, not at Dunadd.

Dr Nora Chadwick, in *The Celts*, makes an important point in distinguishing between 'essential' and 'nonessential' aspects of war. Where territory was not threatened, she remarks:

'This type of warfare had characteristics more akin to those of hunting than to true wars of aggression or defence.'

She links this to the tradition of Gaelic legend, especially the famous *Táin Bó Cuailnge*, or 'Cattle Raid of Cooley', and the exploits of the educated young warriors of the Fianna. The young men of the 'warrior' class, with plenty of energy and nothing productive to do, needed exercise. The raid, designed to lift cattle or slaves, appears to have been a well-established tradition in the societies of third-century Scotland. It was the slave-raiding by the Picts that St Patrick expostulated against in his letter to Coroticus; 100 years later, Columba saw a Scots slave girl at the court of king Bridei. Some writers believe that a newly created king or subking was required by tradition to lead his hunter-warriors off on a raid, whose success would make an auspicious beginning to his reign (a practice certainly known in the Gaelic territories until the 16th century). Such activities were very different from warfare. In the early years of the fifth century, Gildas complains that the Picts are unwilling to face proper warfare, meaning a Roman army, and he was undoubtedly right. Their deep raids into Britannia in the fifth century were entirely opportunistic, based on the lack of defence within the Roman provinces at that time.

The legends of Cuchulainn and other outstanding warriors show that the Gaels placed emphasis on the concept of the champion. Not all warriors were equal. Sometimes the outcome of a dispute would be tried by battle between only two, or a select few, rather than by armies; with the armies drawn up to watch. The bravest or most successful was rewarded with bardic praise and a place close by the king, and also with the champion's portion – the first and biggest joint of meat out of the cooking pot. The similarity of this practice to the contests and feasts described by Homer in the *Iliad* has often been noticed, and some scholars have suggested that such Homeric echoes were late embellishments put in by the twelfth-century scribes, to add greater lustre to their own ancient tales. But, if later Scottish practice between the twelfth and fourteenth centuries is anything to go by, then some issues were indeed fought out by champions, either as single warriors or in small groups, rather than by whole armies. This was not, however an exclusively, 'Celtic' practice.

Among the main sources of names and dates for the period between the fifth and twelfth centuries are the 'Annals', or annual records compiled in Irish and Scottish monasteries. Written in Latin or Gaelic, or a combination of both, none of these survives in original form, but only in copies made at later dates. The oldest manuscript set is the 'Annals of Innisfallen', which were partly compiled around the end of the eleventh century. The chief sources are the 'Annals of Tigernach' from the 14th century and the 'Annals of Ulster' from the 15th. These documents were not compiled from any single source, though it is believed they shared one major single source document, now lost, which is known as the 'Ulster Chronicle'. The 'Annals of Ulster', whose records start from 431, have numerous later additions to the text, made by other scribes, from documents presumably not available to the original writer. The so-called 'Annals of Tigernach' have been shown to have nothing to do with Tigernach, an eleventh-century abbot of Clonmacnoise in Ireland. They begin at 488 and end in the twelfth century, though there is a large gap between mid-766 and mid-974, due to the loss of one of its folio books. Its original text probably began with the Creation story. The 'Annals of Innisfallen', whose text is fragmentary, probably also began at the very beginning, but the surviving text does not go back before Abraham. The notional 'Ulster Chronicle' would seem to have begun at 431 with the Christian mission of Palladius to Ireland, and to have concerned itself with events after Ireland had been converted to Christianity. Its own information is reckoned to have come from the monasteries of Bangor (Co. Down), Iona, and Clonmacnoise, though, from around 673, Applecross (founded from Bangor) could also have been a source of information from Pictland. Although 'Tigernach' and 'Ulster' cover much of the same information, each has details not contained in the other.

The king lists, or regnal lists, are, with the 'Annals', the main source of names and dates in the history of Scotland up to 1034. Royal pedigrees were considered to be of special importance. As with the 'Annals' we have no original records but, from the eleventh century and later, there survive a number of copies made from earlier king lists. The oldest of these is known as the 'Irish Synchronisms', or sometimes 'The Synchronisms of Flann Mainistrech', after their compiler, Flann of Monasterboice. This document, which has two versions, of differing lengths, was intended to list all the kings of the Irish provinces (including Scottish Dàl Riada), grouping them within periods. Flann used several different lists in his compilation.

For Wales, the prime sources are 'The History of the Princes' and the 'Annals of Cambria' – *Brut y Tywysogion* and *Annales Cambriae*, – the main parts of the sparse set of ancient documents that record Welsh history in early medieval times. As the titles suggest, 'The History of the Princes' is in Welsh, and the 'Annals' in Latin. Texts of the 'History' are preserved in three Welsh versions, made in the 13th century from a now lost Latin original. It records events between the years 680 and 1282; while entries for the earlier centuries are brief, often no more than a sentence, those for the eleventh century onwards are much more detailed, though still covering the same type of events. These are battles, royal accessions and deaths, and the appointments and deaths of bishops and abbots, interspersed with occasional terse notes of plagues, eclipses, earthquakes, and exceptionally hot summers and cold winters. The 'Annals' date from around 1100; briefer than 'The History of the Princes', they cover events from 447 to 954, and so the two records frequently give the same information. The existing versions are copies of an original that was itself probably compiled from several different sources.

The Irish Gaels' law system, at least in its later stages, is well recorded. The laws were administered by officials of the druidical or priestly class and they were, at least in earlier times, independent of the king, although the king had to dispense justice according to the laws. In Scotland, mention of the 'laws of Aedh Find' suggests more involvement on the king's part by the eighth century, unless his name is brought in merely to denote the era in which they were drawn up, or to emphasise that these were independent laws of the Scots. However, the way society was organised implies a definite role for the lawmen. From the individual family onwards, the structure of society was tribal, governed by kinship. A group of *tuatha*, or local tribes, combined to form a subkingship; all the subkings owed allegiance to a higher king. Thus, the provinces of Ireland and the *cinele* of the Scottish Gaelic kingdom were arranged. The king of Scots, as we have seen, was the king also of a *cineal*, usually that of Gabhrain, but sometimes that of Loairn. While a king might act impartially among his own people, he would not be expected to be impartial in a dispute involving another *tuath* or *cineal*. A trained man of law, omniscient on all questions of precedent and procedure, his person inviolate by sacred tradition, was needed to ensure that impartial justice was exercised. In early Ireland, such a person was a *brehon* (*breithem* in Old Irish). He was not a judge but an expert available for consultation. The 'brehon laws' recorded in texts from around the end of the sixth century and later, were not an encyclopedic collection of statutes or judgments and give no indication of the underlying legal theory.

The law was not the all-embracing thing it is today. Other powerful regulatory systems operated within society. Custom and superstition were both more deeply entrenched than they are today. In druidic times, the worst penalty for a wrongdoer was to be excluded from the rites; effectively, this turned the person out of the *tuath* and its protection. In the Christian period, excommunication by the Church had the same effect, another feature of life that would continue to produce vagrants and 'broken men' into the 16th century. The adoption of Christianity had some influence on the law, though much of it relates to the position of the clergy; the old custom of permitting multiple wives and easy divorce was enshrined in law for a long time after the Church was established. The laws existed to enforce what was deemed important to the community at the time or, possibly, given the conservatism of such systems, what had been important to its grandparents. Thus the ownership of cows and other livestock, public behaviour, and homicide are all of great prominence.

Each subkingdom was a separate legal jurisdiction, and probably each had a judge, or a number of judges, who officiated on behalf of the king in all but great or disputed cases. There was no great hierarchy and no concept of 'the Law' as a force against wrongdoing. It was up to individuals to invoke it, if they felt wronged. In most cases, compensation was awarded if there was a case to answer. The extent of this depended on the nature of the offence and the status and wealth of the parties involved. Each individual had his 'honour price' (the word used for honour, *enech*, means, literally, 'face') and the fine would be based on that, with an additional body price payable in the case of murder. Both parties had to pledge a surety before the case was heard, and agree to accept the verdict. If a defendant was unable to pay the decreed fine, his kin were required to pay it for him, beginning with his closest relatives but extending to all male descendants of a great-grandfather. Fines were normally payable in the form of cows. In this way, the kin group assumed both control of and responsibility for the actions of its individual members. Failure of a guilty man to pay the fine, or to repay his kin group when he could do so, could result in the loss of his legal rights, which made it legally possible for his opponent to kill him or to have him killed. Incidentally, the importance of the kin group in respects such as this which went on for centuries, does a great deal to explain the interest in pedigree and genealogy which is still often notable in Wales and the other 'Celtic' lands: the identity of one's great-grandfather could be a matter of real importance.

Despite the provisions for restitution and fines, the blood feud between families was a recognised institution. In return for a death or a deadly insult, honour and prestige required satisfaction. The key element was the family or wider kindred. An insult to one was an insult to all; the murder of one might be avenged by all. This of course was the situation that the laws existed to prevent, but it did not always work.

Nora Chadwick, in *The Celts*, draws attention to the institution of *galnes* (known in later Welsh as *galanas*), 'satisfaction for slaughter', among the Britons of Strathclyde, fixing payments to be made by the kin group. She also notes a post-eleventh-century compilation, *Leges Inter Brettos et Scottos*, 'Laws Between the Britons and Scots', based on laws pertaining to the Cumbrian province. By that time, of course, Strathclyde was being drawn into the polity of greater Scotland, and glosses on law and custom would have been essential for those who were in charge of bringing the different systems together.

Once imported to Scotland, the Irish laws may have followed a separate line of development. Certainly the Scots were capable of innovation, the most famous example being the 'Law of Innocents' proposed by abbot Adamnan of Iona in the late seventh century and brought to fulfilment by him at the Synod of Birr in Ireland in 697. This law was intended to exclude women and children from all warfare. Although its main aim was clearly to protect innocent victims, it is likely that it also forbade a practice that had been going on for centuries, that of women warriors. The tradition of this goes a long way back; reference has already been made to how, in the 'Ulster Cycle' legends, Cuchulainn and other heroes were trained in warfare by Scathach, at her school for young warriors in Skye. The law was ratified by 40 senior clerics and 51 rulers, including king Bridei macDerilei of the Picts and Eochaid, king of Scot, as well as many subkings and chiefs. A note in the 'Annals' confirms its renewal in 727, when the saint's bones were transferred to Ireland. In fact, it partook of the nature of an international convention, rather than a traditional type of law. Its specific clauses and sanctions are not known. In a society that still retained and celebrated various forms of violence, it was a notable step forward, reflecting both the pastoral work of the Church and the ability of the leaders to accept change. They may, of course, as reformers often are, have been well ahead of popular opinion, if such a thing can be said to have existed in the seventh century. The notion of the battling woman, like Black Agnes of Dunbar in the 14th century, Grace O'Malley in the 16th, and Marged uch Ifan in the 18th, would continue to be much appreciated by the Scots, Irish, and Welsh.

From references made to king Oengus's imposition of Pictish laws on the conquered Scots of Dàl Riada in the mid-eighth century, it is clear that the Picts had a law system and that was not identical to that of the Scots. What the laws were and how they were administered is not known. From the way in which contemporary references are framed, as 'laws of the Picts', it can reasonably be supposed that there was a general law code accepted throughout Pictish-inhabited territory and interpreted by figures comparable with the *brehons* of Irish tradition, who maintained and, perhaps, also gave judgment. In this respect, there is no reason to suppose that the customs of the Picts were notably different to those of the Scots, except perhaps in the law of land occupancy. Pictish place names, as has been noted, often display a concern with land areas, boundaries, and natural features. Land division, especially in countryside like that of Easter Ross, where the fertile coastal strip may be only one or two miles wide in places, was a vital matter. In addition, the taxation system was based on animals and produce, enhancing the value of good land. Laws defining and protecting tenure were necessary. Business transactions of other kinds and personal misdemeanours also had to be regulated or dealt with.

CHAPTER TWELVE

The Decline and Fall of the Britons

Estimates of the Celtic-speaking population of the Romano-British provinces around the year 411 hover about the million mark. A great nation might have been in the making from those elements plus the imperial tradition, but the Britons were not to be left on their own to create one. On all sides, they were surrounded by hostile peoples who had come to regard the old Roman provinces as a treasure trove. Raiders came from Ireland, from Caledonia, from across the North Sea and the Channel, time and time again. The Britons did not yield tamely, and fought back. A century of crowded, chaotic, and almost unrecorded events filled the Roman power vacuum. What were later to be known as the Dark Ages had arrived. Through those years, two long-term facts became clear. One was that the Britons were not a people with a natural tendency to unity. Despite their common language and their long experience of central government, the old tribal structure still pervaded their attitudes. Mutual hostility and shifting alliances among themselves weakened their capacity to fight back. The other deeply ominous trend, for the Britons, was that the invaders from across the North Sea were not coming merely to raid, or to offer their services as mercenaries. They were intent on settling in the fertile lands of southeast and east Britain, and claiming them as their own.

Long identified as three great groups, the Angles, Jutes, and Saxons, they spilled across from a great swathe of the northwest European coastlands. Their coming was part of a vast migratory movement from northern Europe lasting for more than 200 years, which brought Germanic-speaking peoples all through the shattered western empire, through Spain and into North Africa. They had never been under Roman rule and were wholly pagan in their religion. A strong tradition associates the success of their invasions with the internal disunity of the island peoples. In the middle of the fifth century, a British war leader emerged whose name or honorific title, *Vortigern*, means great chief. To sustain his efforts, either against Picts and Scots or against other Britons, he obtained the services of continental mercenaries under the leadership of two chiefs, Hengest and Horsa. This was in 449. By 455, Hengest and Vortigern were at war with each other. Meanwhile, the continental colonists were settling, Oisc, son of Hengest, is recorded as the first king of Kent. In 477, a Saxon warlord, Aelle, landed on the south coast and established a bridgehead, which was progressively enlarged into Sussex, land of the South Saxons. Further west, in 495, another group landed to form the nucleus of the kingdom of Wessex. The name of its leader, Cerdic, is believed to be British, which suggests that even at this stage there was intermarriage between ruling families of the Saxons and Britons, perhaps as a result of peace treaties or territorial negotiations. As often seen later, royal families seemed to have a gift for placing themselves, as a special social group, above the tribal or national struggles. Other invading-migrating bands sailed up the Thames and Humber estuaries, and into the Wash, and moved inland by river and land, establishing the kingdom of Mercia, its name meaning 'borderland'. Although little detail of individual events is known, the expansion of all these protokingdoms was achieved against fierce British opposition.

The Romano-British tradition records the leader Ambrosius Aurelianus, *Emrys Wledig* in Old Welsh, who appears to have successfully fought the invaders, perhaps in the Somerset marshes. Gildas saw him as 'the last of the Romans' and the name Aurelianus suggests an attempt to make a link with the defunct, but not forgotten, imperial tradition. It is now thought likely that there were two Emryses, father and son. At some point early in the fifth century, the younger Emrys may have fought in a battle whose fame was long preserved in Celtic Britain, the fight at Mount Badon, a site now unknown. It was a British victory, which deterred further expansion of the Anglo-Saxon kingdoms for about 50 years and would have brought immense prestige to the British leader. For a time, there was even a reverse of the occupation process, with groups of the invaders returning to Europe and settling Frisia on the Dutch coastal fringe. But, in the west, there was also a loss of population, as British Celtic speakers, either displaced or fearing displacement or an even worse fate, migrated into Armorica and gave their name to Brittany, which was to remain an independent duchy until the 15th century. With them went, or developed, the tales that would later be blended into the Arthurian tradition, of links between the kingdoms of Brittany and Cornwall.

But the Anglo-Saxon conquest was interrupted, not halted. By 550, the encroachment was again in full force. A strategic battle was fought at Dyrham, near the Roman ruins of *Aquae Sulis* (Bath), in 577 when Ceawlin, king of Wessex, and Cuthwine defeated the Britons and isolated the Britons of the southwestern peninsula. By the turn of the sixth century, most of lowland England was divided into a mosaic of Anglo-Saxon kingdoms or statelets, dominated by warlords. In the northeast, two Anglian states were battling against the indigenous inhabitants for land and existence: Deira, based on York, and Bernicia, based on the fortified rock of Bamburgh. From 588, these were fused into a single Northumbrian kingdom, under the rule of Aethelfrith. The Northumbrians forced their way across into Celtic Cumbria and cut off the Britons north of the old Roman wall from those to the south. Another crucial battle, at Chester, around 616, destroyed the army of the northern Welsh peoples under Solomon, son of Cynan, king of Powys. To the Celts, one of the most horrific aspects of this defeat was the slaughtering by the Northumbrians, before the battle, of the monks of Bangor, who had come, presumably, to encourage the fighting men. This evokes earlier memories of the role played in war by the druids and druidesses of Anglesey. By around 620, British kingdoms survived only in Dumnonia (Devon and Cornwall; resistance to the West Saxons continued here until around 710), Wales, and Strathclyde. Outside the southwest, perhaps the last redoubt of a British monarchy in what was rapidly becoming truly England, land of the Angles, was the kingdom of Elmet, reaching back from the head of the Humber estuary into the Pennines, its location still found in a few place names, like Sherburn-in-Elmet. Its last king was recorded as Cerdic. A personal motive has been ascribed in Bede's history to its conquest, in that a great-nephew of Edwin, who had followed Aethelfrith as king of Northumbria, had died of poison while a guest at Cerdic's court. But, especially in the reign of Edwin, the first Anglo-Saxon king to exercise a degree of rule both north and south of the Humber, the continued independence of Elmet, separating these regions, must have appeared anomalous and undesirable.

How far the Britons survived as an element of the population in the conquered lands is not clear. The Anglo-Saxons were much greater in number than the Romans, who conquered before them, or the later Normans, but it is not likely that they were numerous enough to swamp the existing inhabitants. In eastern England, mass graves have been found with beheaded bodies, but these may have been from reprisals or executions, rather than ethnic massacres. A reduction to slave status was a more probable fate. Many Britons must have fled westwards as a result of eviction, or in fear of death or slavery; the Anglo-Saxon word for 'Briton' also meant 'slave'. Few Brittonic words were adopted into the Anglo-Saxons' language, and though many river and hill names remained Brittonic, and the names of Roman city sites were preserved, the invaders bestowed their own names on their settlements. There is evidence of British survival in some Anglo-Saxon place names, like Bretby (Britons' town), or the many Waltons (strangers' town); the name is found even within Wales, as well as in some preserved laws of Wessex from around 700, which deal with British land-holders. Generally speaking, it is likely that the remnant of British population in Anglo-Saxon England was least in the east and southeast, and the proportion increased towards west and southwest. The language, culture, and religion of the Britons were all eclipsed. In the case of language, what happened in England is quite different from other former Roman provinces of the west. France and Spain, despite being overrun and extensively settled by Franks and Goths, lost their Celtic speech but preserved Latin-based languages. English is, however, a Germanic language, and its substantial French-Latin element comes from later times.

The nature of the Welsh kingdoms of this time is shrouded in obscurity, which the accounts of later chroniclers do not greatly illuminate. As the dynasties grew in power and rivalry, their own propaganda tried to make them as grandly established as possible. Magnus Maximus plays a part in many of these genealogies, indeed John Davies says in *A History of Wales* that:

'In the history or the mythology of the beginnings of the kingdoms of Wales, Magnus is a ubiquitous lurker . . . perhaps it is not overfanciful to consider 383 as the year of the conception of the Welsh nation and to accept Magnus Maximus as the father of that nation.'

By the middle of the sixth century, a number of Welsh kingdoms can be identified. Gwynedd, comprising Anglesey and part of the mainland across the Menai Strait, with its king Maelgwn, was already a significant power. In the southwest, the name of the Demetae remained current for a long time in what was to become the kingdom of Dyfed; Gildas refers to his contemporary Gwrthefyr as 'ruler of the Demetae'. On the north coast, the name of the Deceangli was preserved in the often-disputed territory of Tegeingl, bordering the River Dee. On the eastern edge, small kingdoms arose in the land of the Cornovii, eventually to coalesce in the kingdom of Powys. In the southeast, another set of kingdoms arose in the one-time territory of the Silures: Brycheiniog, Glywysing, and Erging (a name long preserved in English as Archenfield). The divisions between these little states were not hard and fast: Erging, based on the Romano-British region of Ariconium, would become part of England from the late eleventh century. Glywysing split into Morgannwg, Gwynllwg, and Upper and Lower Gwent. The destiny of a kingdom depended on the strength of its people, on the vigour and ability of its king, and, not least, on the chance of whether he had sons or daughters, brothers or sisters, to maintain his own family line.

It may be asked why, following this account of relatively large-scale migration and invasion, we should be sceptical of the same sort of thing happening earlier. There are several answers to this question. Firstly and most importantly, the evidence is there, in both documentary and archaeological form, for the sixth-century invasions. By this time, too, the population of Europe was very much greater than it had been a millennium earlier. The need for land was greater than ever before. The collapse of the western empire made it possible for population movement to happen on a wide scale, unimpeded by the presence of Roman legions. At this time, there was no sense of national boundaries or nation-states; the concept of nationhood was scarcely realised. Although we see in the Irish legends the evidence of profound attachment to the land itself, the germ of national awareness was concentrated in the sense of a people with shared characteristics in culture and a common language, not with a single political system. There could be a multiplicity of rulers – we see this very clearly in the Gaelic kingdoms of Ireland and Scotland, as well as in the kingdoms of Wales, where the feeling of compatriotism did not dispel local rivalries. Nor did the invasions and great folk movements of this period replace the kind of processual change that had occurred before; this process continued and was responsible for the erosion of Pictish in northern Scotland and, in part, for the disappearance of Cumbric in southern Scotland and northern England.

As a result of the Roman occupation, the ancestral form of modern Welsh took in many Latin loan words, most of which have come through into modern Welsh. Such words show how much the Welsh tribes learned from the Romans, and the areas in which the two sides came into contact. Military engineering terms, like *ffos*, (trench), *pont* (bridge), *castell* (castle), form one area. Writing is another, with *llyfr* (book), *llythyr* (letter), and *ysgrif* (script), among others. The Romans' superiority in architecture and building is shown by the borrowing of such words as *ffenestr* (window), *ystafell* (chamber), and *colofn* (pillar). Many domestic items, such as *cyllell* (knife), *ffiol* (bowl), *cannwl* (candle), come from Latin. *Cadair* (throne) is another borrowing but, unlike the Gaels, the Welsh did not use the Latin *rex* for king, retaining instead the traditional *brenin*. As Sir John Lloyd pointed out in 1911, although popular speech may employ Latin-derived words like *pobl* (people) and *estron* (foreigner), the language of Welsh law, belonging to an older and specially preserved tradition, has very few Latin terms other than *tyst* (witness).

For the Britons, the century and a half between 550 and 700 was an era of disaster. Across almost all of England, they were defeated, ousted, enslaved. The shade of Gildas might have taken a dismal satisfaction in the outcome of his prophecy. Though Wales and Strathclyde remained independent, the collective shock and sense of cumulative catastrophe, the feeling of confinement to a vastly reduced territory, the presence of hostile neighbours, perhaps a fear of divine abandonment, must have been very great. In the literature of early Wales can be detected some of the reaction to this condition: anger, dreams of revenge, dwelling on and mourning for past glories and tragedies. An interesting example occurs in the story of the other Emrys Wledig, set in the times when Vortigern was struggling against the first invaders. He is building a fort in the southern reaches of Snowdonia, but finds that the building materials vanish, and new towers and walls collapse every night. Magicians, not priests, surround the leader, and their answer to the problem is to make a human sacrifice to secure the foundations. The blood of a 'fatherless boy' is needed. Such a boy is found in the person of one Emrys, but he is no ordinary child. He confronts the chieftain, and is able to outargue the magicians. He alone knows that under the base of the fortress is a cavern with a pool. Here two dragons do perpetual battle. One is red, representing the Welsh, and one white, representing the Saxons. Vortigern places the fortress in charge of the magical boy; its ruins still have the name of Dinas Emrys. The tale is closely related to others that anticipate the day when Emrys will go to war and sweep the Saxons back into the sea.

The story is first told in the *Historia Brittonum* and repeated with embellishments by a later writer, Geoffrey of Monmouth. Not a lot is known about his life; 'of Monmouth' is how he referred to himself. Born some time before 1100, he lived until 1155. He was a churchman, based for a considerable part of his life in Oxford and, in 1152, he was made bishop of St Asaph in Wales. In the writing of his *Historia Regum Britanniae*, 'History of the Kings of Britain', he claimed to have had the use of a 'very ancient book written in the British [Welsh] language'. There is no supporting evidence for this claim, which is not taken seriously. Geoffrey has been described as 'the inventor of British history', being the first writer to attempt to combine the known elements into a coherent narrative. Unfortunately, 'invention' also applies to most of his content. His book purports to be the history of Celtic Britain from its supposed foundation by a band of Trojans escaping their city's destruction, and led by Brutus (not the Roman Brutus), through 99 kings to Cadwaladr, son of Cadwallon, who died in 689. These two are fully historic figures. But Geoffrey gives a major role to a figure who would otherwise scarcely rate a footnote in history, king Arthur, the great hero of pre-Saxon Britain, with his wizard-counsellor Merlin. He is obliquely mentioned in the 'Gododdin', where a certain warrior is referred to as 'no Arthur', and also figures sketchily in the *Historia Brittonum*. The 'Annals of Cambria' provide the only other mentions of Arthur prior to Geoffrey of Monmouth. Two entries refer to him as taking part in the Battle of Mount Badon

(516) and the Battle of Camlan, in which he was killed (537).
Geoffrey, however, describes his career in detail. His Arthur is a
British monarch – the word 'Celtic' does not occur – whose
empire ultimately covers not only Britain, but Ireland, Iceland,
Norway, Denmark and Gaul. Finally defeated and grievously
wounded, he is taken to Avalon and laid to rest.

Geoffrey's book marks the start of a torrent of Arthurian literature, with much later detail – including the Round Table,
the incorporation of the Grail legend, and all the panoply of
late medieval knighthood – added by other writers, and has
given medieval and modern European literature one of its
greatest themes. Despite some scepticism even at the time the
first copies were circulated (the contemporary writer and traveller, Giraldus Cambrensis, being one unbeliever), it was not
until the 16th century that the facts of Geoffrey's version were
seriously questioned and, even 200 years later, he still influenced wishful thinkers. Writing in an age when fake pedigrees
and imaginary episodes 'reinforcing' truth were common, he
may have been deliberately seeking to glorify the native Welsh
tradition, at a time when Norman rule was being imposed on
his country. Ironically, his 'British' king has long been thor-
oughly accommodated into the ethos and tradition of Anglo-
Saxon England. Despite diligent archaeological work at sites
such as Tintagel and Cadbury, and a wide range of speculative
writing that tends to assume the reality of Arthur, and to claim
him variously for Dumnonia, Wales, and Scotland, no satisfactory evidence about his existence has ever appeared. Like the
ancient Irish and Welsh legends, the Arthurian romances are
like a fascinating forest-land, full of gaudy castles, enchanted
lakes, extraordinary beasts, and more-than-human people.
Their purpose, symbolism, and mythical roots can be end-
lessly debated by scholars and enthusiasts, but, though their
'Celtic' origin is indisputable, they have nothing to contribute
to any understanding of sixth-century events and people in
England, Wales, and Scotland.

CHAPTER THIRTEEN

Before the Storm

There is no doubt that the peoples of the British Isles were 'Celtic' even before the label was given to the continental Celts, and that the same is true of the continental peoples themselves. But what does Celtic mean in this context? Only that similar languages were spoken and that there is no significant known break in the continuity of habitation on either side. The archaeologist, Simon James, in a book provocatively entitled *The Atlantic Celts: Ancient People or Modern Invention?* writes:

> 'There never was a pristine cultural or ethnic identity ('Celtic' or anything else) across the archipelago, but always multiple traditions, undergoing contest and change.'

James, a strong adherent of the no-invasions theory, even rejects the identity conferred by Celtic language, not because it is false but because he feels it cannot now be separated from the illusive notion of a Celtic 'race' that came to populate the islands. He says, surely rightly, that there was no island-wide notion of ethnic 'Britishness' or 'Irishness' either, let alone awareness of overarching 'Celticness'. The inhabitants of the islands, in independent and largely self-sufficient communities based on family and kinship, had no need to seek wider identities. This would not prevent them from speaking similar languages, or even forms of the same language, and from engaging in trade and exchange both with closer and more distant communities, depending on their needs and what they had to offer. It certainly would not deter them from making war on one another.

A wide-scale climate fluctuation is recorded around 536–45, just into the second generation of the Dàl Riadan colonisation. Sally Foster describes this period as years of 'plague, appalling weather and famine across Europe (including Ireland)', assessed from observation of tree rings, and suggests the effects of meteorite impact as a possible cause. Little human evidence of this has been found in Ireland or Scotland, but it was a time of great upheaval, though poorly recorded, in England. Gildas describes what seem to be genuine plague symptoms. But after this period, a slow progress of climatic improvement began. This gradually also increased the extent of cultivable land available to the inhabitants. It may have contributed to the rise in population in Scandinavia, which helped to produce the Viking expansion, and it undoubtedly assisted them in their seaborne attacks and invasions (it was from the Hebridean Norse colony that Iceland was colonised).

While the travails of the Britons from invasion and war went on through the sixth and seventh centuries, Ireland remained inviolate. Hibernia, it seems, lay beyond one sea too many, or too far, for the continentals. The Irish were also fortunate in that the western shores and harbours were held by the Britons, and so the British island did not form a stepping stone to their own green pastures. In a manner unparalleled elsewhere in Europe, Irish society developed on its own during four-fifths of the first millennium CE, untroubled by external forces. The 100 or so petty tribal units, with their fluid incorporation into overkingdoms and provincial kingdoms, continued to be the basis of political organisation. The rath, the crannog, and the turf hut continued to be the homes of the people. The only great new element was the Church, which was itself adapted to the tribal structure of society. But it brought in the study of Latin and Greek, and the practice of writing, pioneered by St Finnian at the monastery of Clonard, and following the example he had seen at St Davids in Wales. The learning of the educated classes was adapted to embrace classical themes as well as Christian theology and social teaching. Large monastic communities appeared during the seventh century at such places as Clonmacnoise, Bangor, Clonfert, and Kildare. Kings were pleased to grant them extensive land and rights; they were wealthy foundations and their abbots men of power and importance in the secular world, as well as the spiritual. With substantial communities of laymen established in conjunction with the abbeys, these places, unwalled and undefended, became the nearest thing to towns that Ireland had yet seen. Christianity also required an outward-directed approach, and this became important when paganism seemed to be triumphant not only in the former Britannia, but across much of northern Europe. If some of the Celtic clergy remained devoted to a hermit life in the far west, others accepted the task of taking the Gospel to the new pagan nations. Missionaries from the Celtic Church played an important part in the renaissance of Christianity in England and central and northern Europe, and maintained links with their parent foundations. Columbanus, who left Bangor, Ireland, in 695, spent the next 25 years founding a series of abbeys in Gaul, Switzerland, and Lombardy, and despite many other disputes and vicissitudes, always had time to defend the Irish tradition of which he was himself a distinguished representative.

Though inviolate, Ireland was, thus, not isolated. Especially in the north, there was an increasing degree of interconnection with the growing and energetic Gaelic kingdom of Dàl Riada. Kings and subkings on both sides had shared and mutual interests and engaged in conferences, alliances, and wars, as the case might be, in the maintenance of their own positions and those of their wider families. The water gap was a highway, rather than a barrier, linking tribally based communities with a common language, religion, and cultural tradition. The general style and level of life, despite the presence of the

Church, had not changed greatly since the early part of the millennium. In *A History of Ireland*, Edmund Curtis wrote that:

> 'By CE800, Ireland had become a unity of civilization and law, and no languages save the Gaelic of the ruling classes and the Latin of the Church were spoken.'

But he had to allow that 'for all that there was little centralized authority'.

Political organisation had advanced to accept the notion of the high king, or *ard rí*, though this title simply defined the most powerful of numerous kings, rather than a generally accepted and codified supraregal role – it was very far from the status of a monarch. Its origins seem to lie with the dynasty of the Uí Néill, who claimed descent from Niall Noígiallach, 'of the Nine Hostages', and of Conn Cétchathach before him, and who ruled from the ancient site of Temair (Tara), in County Meath. This was a place of importance from at least Neolithic times, and its earliest king was said to be the god Lug himself. In the third century, one of its kings was Cormac macAirt, in whose reign the exploits of Finn macCumhaill and the Fianna were said to have taken place. Many traditions lay around the kingship of Tara, and the concept of *fir flathemon*, 'justice of a ruler', was one which went far back, perhaps to Cormac or even earlier. Among Irish kings, the ruler of Tara possessed a prestige and special status, which the Uí Néill exploited to claim primacy, but there is no evidence that they were able to exercise any kind of sovereignty in the seventh and eighth centuries.

During this 'Dark-Age' phase, in the seventh and eighth centuries, the disruption of life across much of England and, in Europe, across France, the Low Countries, and into Germany, caused by invasion, war, and folk movements, must also have destroyed or gravely impaired trading links that had long been established. From this period, there is very little evidence to be gleaned of trading from the 'Celtic' lands, at least until the consolidation of Frankish power under Charlemagne in the late

eighth century, and the rise to dominance of the Anglo-Saxon
kingdom of Mercia in Middle England, began to create conditions of greater stability. Currency in the form of an official
coinage was not found necessary by the tribal kingdoms in
Scotland, Ireland, and Wales, and they must have subsisted on
their own resources. These, in the later Iron Age, were probably quite sufficient in essentials. Ample supplies of timber, fisheries, grazing, and arable land, were all still available. Iron
technology and deposits of bog ore, combined with copper,
lead, and silver mining, ensured that tools and weapons could
be made. Salt was being extracted by the panning process in a
number of coastal locations. But during this period also began
the custom of pilgrimage to Rome. This long and often haz-
ardous overland journey had previously been made only by senior clerics concerned with the affairs of the Church, but now
other members of the upper level of society might undertake it
as part of their personal religious life.

The sense of Gaelic supratribal identity, which had arisen in
Ireland, extended into Dàl Riada, the Gaelic kingdom of western Scotland. But that land also held two other sets of inhabitants: the Britons of Strathclyde and the Picts of the north. By
547, the Northumbrians controlled the region of Lothian.
Around 603, the Scots, under a dynamic and ambitious king,
Aedan, went to war with the Northumbrians but were defeated
at a site known as Degsasatan, in the Borders. Through the first
half of the seventh century, there were recurrent battles
between Picts and Scots. Anglian attempts, from Northumbria,
to push their dominion beyond the Firth of Forth on the eastern side were decisively defeated by the Picts under Nechtan
macBili at the crucial battle of Dunnichen, in Angus, in 685.
This event, combined with their possession of more than half
the mainland territory, suggests that the Picts, at this time, were
dominant among the three northern peoples.

Columcille had died in 597 but his great prestige and his
monastery's established role ensured that Iona remained the

spiritual centre of the Church (though such a claim, if made, would certainly have been disputed by larger abbeys like Clonmacnoise). Part of Iona's importance lay in the fact that the Picts, once they became Christian, long accepted it as their religious centre, and the priests and monks of Pictland were trained there. The power and effectiveness of Pictish monarchy is likely to have fluctuated, as also happened with the kingship of Scots and the overkingships of Ireland. A strong king and good fortune might see a period, as with Oengus between 729 and 761, when his rule extended over the entire territory of the Picts, and from 741, exercised hegemony over the Scots as well. Vigorous local leaders and internecine disputes could also bring times when the Pictish kingdom was virtually fragmented into its provinces.

The northern tribes had shown an ability to combine in emergency, from the days of Calgacus to the defeat of the Northumbrian king Ecgfrith at Dunnichen. But, by the early seventh century, their world looked less stable than it had 100 years before. The Scots were by now a substantial people – the evidence of the *Senchus Fer nAlban* suggests they were subdivided, in islands and mainland, into seven major groups – and Pictland was the natural place for them to expand into. The kingdom of Strathclyde was less attractive to them because of Northumbrian interests there. In Galloway, the ancient church foundation at Whithorn had been brought into the Anglian scheme of things, and made subject to the bishop of Durham; the position after 685 is less clear, though Sir Frank Stenton, writing in *Anglo-Saxon England*, was of the opinion that:

' . . . it is improbable that Galloway or any part of the Solway coast was in their [Strathclyde] hands. Within fifty years of Ecgfrith's death, Whithorn, the most famous church of Galloway, had become the seat of an English bishopric, and one of the greatest of Northumbrian crosses had been erected at Ruthwell near Dumfries.'

The Strathclyde Britons played no part at Nechtansmere, and the Pictish ascendancy is likely to have pushed them back inside their old frontiers, leaving the southern fringe of Galloway under strong Northumbrian influence and perhaps actual control.

In earlier times, the centre of Pictish kingship was in the north, in or near Inverness, but, by around 700, it had moved south, into Angus or Strathearn. Several reasons have been put forward for this shift. It may reflect a political need to control a province with overindependent rulers. Perhaps it shows the expansion of a set of family interests based originally in the north, or the opposite – the rise of a southern family eclipsing a northern one. The southern frontier of the Picts was clearly still at risk from the Northumbrians and may have required the authority and resources of the king to help maintain it. There was a further good reason. To Pictish strategists, the threat of a northward push from the Cineal Loairn must have seemed a minor one compared with the strong eastward-bearing pressures initiated by Aedan towards Atholl, Strathearn, and Strathmore. The name of Atholl, not only Gaelic but proclaiming an identity of 'New Ireland' first noted from 739, shows a Scottish identity proclaimed in a Pictish province long before Kenneth MacAlpin's time. By 770, the Scots had thrown off Pictish rule, and reinstituted their own laws, associated with the name of king Aedh Find.

The lawgiving Aedh Find died around 778 and was followed by his brother Fergus, who ruled for three years. After Fergus, the line of kingship is hard to trace until the appearance of Kenneth MacAlpin, about 60 years later. It has been suggested that there was no single king of the Scots during this period. Such disunity would certainly have provided an opportunity for a Pictish king to re-establish Oengus's dominion over the Scots. But the Picts, too, were in disarray. After the death of their king Ciniod in 775, there may have been a period in which the Picts had no overking whose control covered the whole extent of

Pictish territory – still the entire northern mainland and the islands. The crucial area was Fortriu, the Pictish province that bordered on Dàl Riada and that had already been substantially settled by Scots. To the south, it abutted on British Strathclyde and Anglian Lothian. This area of mixed population could well claim to be the crucible in which Scotland's future was moulded. One of the Pictish kings of the time, Talorcan or Dubtolargg, 'dark Talorcan', is noted in the 'Annals of Ulster' as 'king of the Picts to the south of the Mounth', implying that his authority did not extend to the north. There was perpetual strife among these petty kingdoms, both within the Scottish and Pictish spheres and between them, but this seems to have masked a significant process of mingling and adoption of a shared identity.

The intermarrying of ruling families of Scots and Picts, combined with the different laws of inheritance in each community, and the existence within each of centripetal tribal loyalties, had combined to create a situation where part-Pictish and part-Scottish rulers and would-be rulers could exercise conflicting claims on either side of the border. In such a situation, the traditional means of ensuring succession through the *derbfine*, tricky enough at any time, must often have been almost unmanageable. A mixed Scottish and Pictish population in the Pictish provinces or subkingdoms of Fortriu (preserving the name of the Verturiones) and Atholl further complicated matters. What was happening meanwhile in the great area of Pictland north and northwest of the Mounth is simply not known. If it was a separate Pictish kingdom or kingdoms at this time, it did not produce any ruler strong enough to impose himself on the disputants of the south. Eventually, from 789, Constantine emerges as the strong man. It appears likely that he combined the kingship of Fortriu with that of Dàl Riada between 811 and his death in 820.

Such a process of intermingling, which eventually must have made it difficult for inhabitants of these populous southern provinces of old Pictland to define themselves as wholly Scot or Pict, is most probably the key to the events which took place after 839, when Kenneth MacAlpin assumed the kingship of the Scots and, around 843, also became king of the Picts. Unlike previous kings who ruled both sets of peoples, he formed them into a single political and religious unit: the core of what, from the tenth century, would be known as Scotland. But this process was also to be driven forward by a powerful external force.

At the start of the last decade of the eighth century, across the Celtic kingdoms, no one, not priests nor prophets, omen-readers, soothsayers, wise women, bards, nor spell-casters, was able warn the people of the impending storm. Neither these nor anyone else had any premonition of the advent of the Norsemen. In 795, they struck from the sea, looting and killing in the undefended monasteries and farmsteads, plundering the Hebrides from Skye to Iona and reaching as far south as Lambay Island, Co. Dublin. No longer was Ireland inviolate. Within a few years, the presence of the Vikings as settlers and colonists had wrought massive changes across both major islands, and would continue to do so into the eleventh century and, through their Norman-French descendants, for centuries after that. With them, in the wake of terror and destruction, came new elements into old societies – towns, trade, currency, a different sort of kingship. Though the incomers would, in time, be Christianised, and partly Gaelicised, and though the societies of Gaelic Ireland and Scotland, and of Welsh Wales, remained in many respects different, and retained much from before the Viking era, the events of the ninth and later centuries altered them and pulled them into the context of a new medieval European world. The appearance of the Vikings marked the beginning of the end of the British kingdom of Strathclyde; it speeded up the union of the Scots and Picts, and created a different Ireland. The island peoples remained, as did their languages, and their hybridised cultures kept plenty of vigour. But, among them, if not so drastically as in England, the Teutonic incursions heralded the end of an immemorial era.

CHAPTER FOURTEEN

The Art of the Island Celts

In the light of what has been said of 'Celtic' origins in the British Isles, is Celtic a meaningful word to use about the art of the islanders? The answer must be 'no', albeit a qualified negative. To most people, the mention of Celtic art will call up a certain mental image. Whether based on carved stone, moulded or inlaid metalwork, or manuscript illustration, it will involve curving lines, arranged in an interlaced pattern and decorated with quirky little details of animal heads, in a blend of the abstract and naturalistic. Any accompanying commentary is likely to include mention of such aspects as fluidity of line, oblique rather than direct representation, a love of intricate patterning, and an appearance of symmetry that, on closer examination, is usually subtly asymmetric. A love of decoration will be mentioned, perhaps along with a cautionary note that what we see as decoration may have a magic or religious significance that is now lost. Whatever we see in the work, we assume – surely correctly – that we will not perceive the depth of symbolic reference and meaning that was evoked in the minds of the artist and the artist's contemporaries. In *The Western Celts*, Venceslas Kruta writes that:

> 'Without this art, it would be difficult today to have much idea of the existence of a specifically Celtic mentality, shared for almost five hundred years by the peoples who inhabited the major part of Europe, from the Atlantic to the Carpathians.'

Although accepting that the Celts never achieved any sort of political empire in Europe, he believes that:

> 'They did, however, achieve a spiritual unity that has survived in the original plastic language they evolved.'

Kruta suggestively links some aspects of this art to a comment made by the Greek writer, Diodorus Siculus, in the first century CE, about the Celts' language, as being 'brief, enigmatic, often hyperbolic, with frequent recourse to implied meanings'. Anyone familiar with spoken or translated Gaelic will know that, as a modern language, it retains something of this oblique and referential quality. But it is a bold assumption to suppose a shared mentality across such a range of peoples and territory over half a millennium.

Much of this decorative aspect is traced to the influence of the La Tène culture of continental Europe, which itself owed a great deal to the manufacturing and design techniques of the Mediterranean region. At this time, there was a broad similarity in art across a wide extant of Europe and the effects of this can be seen in the British Isles. The most typical form is the 'vegetal' style, of scroll designs based on leaf and flower patterns, like the acanthus and lotus, developed. Practice of this was aided by the use of compasses, enabling the designer to form a pattern of circles and part-circles. The islanders took to the use of compasses with enthusiasm, though they added their own stylistic features to the designs, elaborating them by intricate cross-hatching, the short incised strokes going in series at right angles to one another in a way which recalls basketwork, or perhaps a form of weaving. But the new methods and new designs were integrated with existing practice. There is no denying the consistency of a tradition that has been traced back by a leading authority to far before the La Tène era. In *Irish Art in the Early Christian Period*, Dr Françoise Henry comments:

'Right through the history of art in Ireland in the first centuries CE there are facts which show a contact with megalithic patterns . . . all this shows over a long period, contacts
with prehistoric art which opens up the way for imitations,
more likely on the whole than simple survivals though these
can never be ruled out altogether.'

Spirals, rings, and maze-like patterns are found carved in
Neolithic tombs in Ireland, northern England, and Scotland.
The patterns of art on rock and stone surfaces are not naturalistic,
but adopt forms that appear abstract or symbolic. Interlacing
patterns may go back to ancient modes of indicating water. The
shimmering effect above a fire, which we understand as dis-
turbed and expanding molecular formations in the air, was
interpreted by prehistoric peoples in a very different way.
Abstract-seeming curvilinear patterns may relate to this. The
'Celtic' influences that came in, much later, from the continent
may have been all the more readily received because of their
correspondence with a very ancient insular tradition. 'Insular',
or at least 'Insular Celtic' art, is a more accurate description of
the artistic and craft styles that ensued. That there was interest
in new designs can be seen from the first-century artefacts
recovered on Lambay Island in Dublin Bay, among which are a
Roman brooch and a local copy of it, cast in a single piece by
the craftsman, so that the pin is integral with the body and cannot be used. But whenever the artefacts and art of the islanders
is examined in detail, it is its differences and the process of
internal development, which become significant.

The versatility and range of insular Celtic art can be seen in
the work of three high-point periods: that of the metalware
produced in the early first century CE, that of the Picts' stone-
carving in the eighth century, and that of the illuminated books
from around the end of the eighth century.

From around 75BCE into the first century CE, British bronze-
workers made and decorated fine mirrors, presumed to be for

the use of members of the social elite groups. The backs of these are decorated in a manner reminiscent of La Tène but with the kind of distinctive insular features noted above, such as cross-hatching in such a way as to emphasise the interplay of light and shade. At the same time, perhaps influenced by Belgic incomers, the use of coloured enamels in the making of both ornamental and functional objects, like harness fittings, reached its peak. Bronze retained its prestige in the creation of such small items. The artists used the method of *cire perdue*, 'lost wax', whereby the article was first modelled in beeswax, which was then set in soft clay and warmed until the wax ran out through a vent. The clay vessel was then baked to produce a mould, in which the bronze could be cast. Enamelling was then applied; originally only red had been used but, by this time, the techniques of preparing blue and yellow were also available, producing objects of fine detail and bright permanent colour. Much other superb metalwork from this period has been discovered. Most spectacular is perhaps the hoard found at Snettisham in Norfolk, then part of the Iceni tribal lands. Over 50 torcs, of gold or electrum (a gold-silver alloy), were found, and assumed either to be from the treasury of a sacred site, or of a ruling dynasty.

When the community generates enough food and wealth to create a surplus, so that it no longer exists on the brink of survival, art and display become possible. In the Scottish north-east, there had been clearly enough of a surplus to allow for production of the high-quality ornamental 'Caledonian' metalwork of the first centuries CE. In the districts where the Pictish carved stones are found, there were evidently sufficient resources for chiefs or kings to be patrons of a rich sculptural tradition that flourished from the seventh to the ninth centuries. Pictish carving is of particular interest because it is in many ways independent of the Insular Celtic tradition, and is the most naturalistic of all British 'Celtic' art. Some Pictish images have a simplicity of line and a reduction to basic shape that make them seem more like products of the 21st century than the seventh. But, in other ways, they can seem intensely remote; Ian Finlay wrote in *Art in Scotland* that:

> ' . . . when we stand before such monuments as the Hilton of Cadboll stone we feel a profound intervening gulf. The artist who carved these horsemen, these priests, those tireless spirals, might have been the servant of Assurbanipal or Darius, so far as any kinship with him is apparent.'

Some of these stones depict scenes that seem to illustrate an actual event. But much of what the stones could tell us is locked up in two impenetrable codes: the Pictish symbols and the Pictish inscriptions. These, both agreed by scholars to be unique, have always been a strong part of the case of those who argue that the Picts were a people of significantly different traditions and customs to their neighbours. By contrast, the detailed findings of modern archaeology in the Pictish region tend to support the notion that the Picts lived in a manner very similar to that of the other peoples of the British Isles. Their houses, utensils and weapons – the material culture – closely resemble those of the Britons and Scots. But the art of these stones is exclusively Pictish. It is also generally agreed, even by non-Scottish experts, that they represent sculptural art of a high order. The 'St Andrews sarcophagus' has been called the finest piece of European art of the Dark Ages.

Stone-carving in Britain, from the second century, often shows a debt to Roman themes, but the sculptures that begin to appear in Pictland from the sixth century show no obvious debt to Roman sources. Although some observers claim to have detected resemblances to late Roman sculpture in subject matter, the style is quite different, and the Pictish stones are found in regions where no Roman sculptures were set up. Cut into undressed stone surfaces, and incised (the sculptured form cut into the stone surface rather than standing out from it in relief), the oldest stones are defined as 'Class I' sculptures in Allen and Anderson's still-definitive survey of 1903. Stones

of this type are most common in Orkney and on the east side
of the mainland as far south as the Firth of Tay. Well over half
the total number are located north of the River Dee. Dr Isabel
Henderson draws the conclusion:

> 'The natural implication is that Class I, and so the practice
> of erecting symbol stones, began in the north.' (*The Picts*)

Despite its logic, this conclusion ignores the possibility that
there were cultural differences between the peoples of Argyll
and the northeast at this time. In the course of the sixth century,
the Picts, in their northern regions, of which so little is known,
and whatever their own domestic strains and upheavals, developed a remarkable school of sculpture. Dr Henderson would
place the starting point of this school around the head of the
Moray Firth; it could even be further north, in Orkney.

Working from the sketchy evidence that exists, Professor
Charles Thomas linked the animal art of the Class I Pictish
stones to similar but more crudely carved Iron Age designs
found in certain caves on the Fife coast and at Covesea in
Moray, and on pottery fragments at Scottish sites. He ascribed
the easily decipherable symbols, like the comb and mirror, to
representations of prestige goods made in the La Tène style.
The geometrical and indecipherable symbols, he suggested,
stemmed from further back in the Bronze Age. The preservation of these symbols from varying degrees of prehistoric
remoteness is ascribed by Thomas to the fact that they corresponded to the designs tattooed or painted upon the Picts themselves. Whether marked on skin or stone, they would share the
same significance. Like earlier theorists, Thomas took the view
that the stones were gravestones – either actual grave markers or
stones commemorating an individual – and that, therefore, the
symbols on the stones described or referred to that person. This
view has had some recent support from archaeology, which has
established that a substantial number, if not all, are close to grave
sites. However, the presence of identical symbols on items like

bone pins and metal plaques, apparently meant for everyday use, suggests that they should not be seen as 'funerary', though they may still relate to social rank and function.

The carving on Pictish stones is far from being a 'folk art'. Like the fine metalwork discovered at Pictish sites like Norrie's Law and St Ninian's Isle, it is clearly aristocratic art and whatever its purpose, or purposes, it served the leaders of society. This is already apparent in the quality of design on Class I stones, and is even more clear in the stones designated as Class II. On these, the sculpture is not incised into a flat surface, but stands out from it in relief. The stone is cut and dressed: that is, it is formed into a rectangular slab, flat-faced on both sides, with a prepared surface from which the sculptural details will stand out. A number of stones, mostly in the Angus region, combine both the incised and the relief techniques, and are seen as transitional between the two main classes. There is no means of knowing whether the significance of the designs, especially those that are purely symbolic, was apparent to everyone in the Pictish community, or whether it represented a semisecret code. But, if they were based on personal decorations, it can be supposed that the meaning was plain to everyone. Many of the Class II stones tell, or seem to tell, a story, with depictions of warriors and of hunting and battle scenes. Many of them also incorporate Christian imagery, and it becomes a standard practice to have double-sided stones with a cross carved on one face, with much interlaced design, and a variety of different elements on the other face. It is notable that the enigmatic symbols, crescents, angled rods, jigsaw-puzzle-like shapes, and so on, continue to appear on stones with primary Christian figures or symbols, suggesting strongly that either the old symbols were not related to religion or they were related in such a way that they could readily be brought within the scope of a Christian set of references.

The distinction between Class I and Class II is not one of time. Although the earliest stones are all of Class I, stones of this type continued to be carved into the time when sculptures

of Class II, with Christian iconography, were also being created. Ogam inscriptions on some Class I stones have been
dated to the eighth century, well into the period of Class II.
Class II stones, much less numerous, are concentrated in the
'southern Pictland' region of Strathearn, Angus, and the
Mearns. Their relative lack in the far north is all the more surprising since two of the finest of all sculptures in this group are
those of Hilton of Cadboll and Nigg, both in Easter Ross and
well to the north of king Bridei's old royal base at Inverness.

The purpose of the stones and their symbols has provoked a
probably endless debate and sparked off much scholarly ingenu-
ity. As long as the meaning of the symbols remains unclear – and
there seems virtually no prospect of this position altering – there
will be theories, but none can ever be objectively proved. Other
peoples, from the Hittites to the Greeks and Romans, used stone
monuments for a variety of purposes: as gravestones, commem-
orative stones, information boards, votive panels in shrines, and
boundary markers – there seems no reason why the Picts, once
they had established a tradition of sculpture, should not have been
equally diverse in their use of sculptured monuments. The survival of the stones and the disappearance of much else is likely to
prejudice our view of their relative importance. Possibly there
was far more wood-carving than stone-carving, but hardly any of
the former would survive. Dr Isabel Henderson says:

' . . . there is no doubt that the Pictish symbols fit most naturally into the context of some kind of system of pagan concepts. But no proof of such a connection is yet forthcoming.'

This remains the case. On the Class II stones, dating from the
post-Christian period, these symbols continue to be used; additional elements in the design are mostly Christian or secular.
Few of these new features can be said to have a specifically pagan
intention, though many are of pagan origin, perhaps copies from
some classical models available to the sculptors: they include
such creatures as centaurs. A particularly interesting example is

an eighth-century stone slab at Meigle, No 22, which shows a small nude figure, sitting apparently cross-legged, though the legs have been turned into a scroll design with fishtail terminations. Its head is horned and, in its upraised hands at each side, it seems to be brandishing coiling snakes. This figure has been related by Dr Anne Ross, in *Pagan Celtic Britain*, to Cernunnos, the horned god of the Celts, lord of the animals. It has a striking resemblance to a figure of the same deity on the first-century silver cauldron discovered at Gundestrup in Denmark and generally accepted as of Celtic workmanship, whose posture is undoubtedly similar, and to other later examples in Ireland. It shows, in one of the most populous areas of Pictland, not far from the royal centre of Scone, and in the century when Pictish Christianity was sufficiently advanced to reject Iona and to turn, via Northumberland, towards Rome, that a continuing strain of paganism was sufficiently strong to be publicly displayed in stone-carving. It is presumed that Christian priests always broke and destroyed the old icons of paganism whenever they found them, but this one was made after Christianity became official. Irrespective of such speculation, if the figure is indeed Cernunnos, it provides evidence of the Picts sharing at least one god with their fellow-Celts, and, therefore, in all likelihood, sharing others as well.

Aside from their aesthetic value and their possible role in the development of 'Dark Age' art in the far northwest of Europe, the main interest of the Pictish carvings is in the light that they shed on the people who produced them, or who sustained the economy that produced them. Even as one accepts that the Picts were, to all intents and purposes, another island people, or group of peoples, established on their territory since Neolithic times, and sharing the basic elements of a society with few real differences (before the Roman invasion) from Land's End to Muckle Flugga, one feels bound to make a few reservations. The Picts undoubtedly did certain things differently from the neighbouring peoples. Although their sculpture is the most concrete evidence of this, there are significant hints of difference in social practices. They themselves cannot have been unaware of these differences and perhaps deliberately accentuated them.

Though it comes just after the period covered by this volume, even as the Pictish carving tradition waned, with the neglect and abandonment of other aspects of Pictish culture, a revived school of sculpture was emerging in Ireland and the former Dàl Riada, with the splendid high crosses, fusing Christian iconography with imagery and stylistic features that hark as far back as La Tène. The high crosses of the ninth century and later almost certainly replace an earlier sculptural tradition in which wood, and wood faced with bronze, were used as well as stone.

Within the period to 800, the great artistic contribution of the monasteries of the Celtic Church was its illuminated Gospels and other manuscripts: an accomplishment which reached its peak just in time, as the Vikings were about to destroy the life and fabric of some of the abbeys most closely associated with such work, notably Lindisfarne and Iona. An element of tug-of-war between later Scottish and Irish – and even English – national pride has sometimes been noticeable in discussions of the two famous illuminated books, of Kells and of Durrow, and where they were made. Was it an Irish monastery? Or Iona? Or – in the case of the Durrow book – Lindisfarne? As they are among the great works of early European art, the possessiveness is understandable. Both now repose in the library of Trinity College, Dublin. The *Book of Durrow* is a small volume, with the Bible text in Latin. Its illustrations show a distinct Saxon influence – hence the claim for Lindisfarne, which had a fine scriptorium – but it has been shown that decorative metalwork in Saxon style was common in Ireland in the late seventh century. The *Book of Kells*, also a Gospel manuscript, is larger in format, with 340 remaining pages. The work of several different artists, it is the most splendid and ambitious work of its period, agreed to be late eighth century to early ninth century.

For the authority on Irish art, Françoise Henry, the important aspect of these books is not their exact provenance, or the dating – 'chronology is not the essential point in a study of Irish illumination' – but the tracing of the artistic tradition they represent, which she states to be indisputably Irish and, in these two cases, certainly from a Columban monastery, whether Derry, Durrow, Kells, Iona, or another.

Perhaps the most poignant manuscript to survive is the *Cathach*, 'Battler': pages of a sixth-century Latin manuscript Psalter written in the time of, and quite possibly by the hand of, Columcille, with whose name it has always been associated. Kept for centuries by the O'Neills and used by them as a totem in battle (hence its name), it is now preserved by the Royal Irish Academy.

These supreme works of art, made over a period of 800 years, across the whole extent of the British Isles, in a variety of media, exhibit both the aspects of continuity and of change and development, of interrelatedness and independence, among the island peoples. Many writers have commented on the consistency of Celtic culture. John Davies points out, with reference to the Welsh, that:

'Their culture had a tenacious longevity. The characteristics of the Celts, as described by the classical authors, can be clearly discerned a millennium later in the laws and the myths of the Irish; half a millennium later still the same characteristics may be seen in the society portrayed in the *Mabinogi*, and in centuries yet later still there is more than an echo of them in the social order praised by the Welsh poets.'

Over an equivalent period, motifs and elements in art recur again and again in a variety of contexts.

Chapter Fifteen

Postscript on the Island Celts

From around the year 800CE, social and political events in the British Isles are increasingly dominated by the influence of the English, Scandinavian, and Norman-French invaders of the sixth, seventh, ninth, tenth, and eleventh centuries. The unified English kingdom sought, almost succeded, and ultimately failed, over almost a millennium, to extend its control throughout Ireland. Its language succeeded where its kings and queens failed, though even this can be disputed. There may be a substantial amount of truth in the suggestion that the Irish took the English language and made it their own, giving up their own traditional speech in the process. The fact that the English authorities wished this to happen and even passed laws to try to make it happen does not mean that they made it happen. A degree of popular consent was necessary. In Ireland, as in Scotland, the use of English was accepted while the political and religious dominion of England was rejected. In Scotland, as in Ireland, a relatively recent sentiment has grown up, to the effect that Gaelic speech was systematically thrashed out of generations of schoolchildren in the 19th century. Though individual cases are attested, this general folk myth has been disproved by Victor Durkacz in *The Decline of the Celtic Languages*, in which he shows how the process of abandonment had been ongoing from the medieval period, and where he sums it up:

'Wherever the languages clashed, English invariably pre-
dominated – a reflection of the economic vigour and cultural buoyancy of the English-speaking peoples.'

The last phrase is very significant: it refers not to the 'English'
but to a much wider group, indeed now a worldwide one,
who, like the 'Celtic' speakers of the centuries preceding the
Common Era, are linked by the use of a common language
and a number of associated cultural links, and who retain separate identities in politics, religion, and a whole variety of
other ways.

Readers who have reached this point will be aware that the
words 'Celt' and 'Celtic' are of little or no value in real
description when it comes to examining the ancient history
of the British Isles and, far from being 'time-honoured', are of
fairly recent origin. As identifiers of some inhabitants of
Britain and Ireland, they are no older than the 18th century
and have no 'racial' meaning of any kind. Their only coher-
ence is with respect to language, where the 'Celtic' tongues
can be shown to have a mutual relationship and a common or
mutuallyshared ancestral language source. In any other
respect, the words can, and do, mean whatever anyone likes.
Although this may distress the authors of numerous books,
which proclaim Celtic achievements, both ancient and modern, and the creators of numerous Celtic web-sites, dedicated
to celebrating a Celtic identity, it is also what enables them to
freely link 'Celtic' to any kind of nebulous or novel concept of
their own.

By means of a sort of temporal paradox, the archaeologist
Simon James suggests that although the notion of 'insular
Ancient Celts' is false, that does not make the modern Celts
bogus – because they 'constitute a true case of "ethnogene-
sis".' He means that, from the 17th century on, these latter-
day Celts fulfil certain requirements that make them a
recognisable and coherent ethnic group:

- 'They have a sense of shared difference, and usually per-
  ceived threat, from another group with which they are in
  contact' (i.e. the English).
- 'They express their identity by attaching symbolic value
  to aspects of their culture deemed characteristic' (e.g. language, or in this case, languages; but perhaps also costume, music, etc.).
- 'They choose an ethnonym' (i.e. a common ethnic name,
  in this case, Celts).
- They 'create an agreed common history' (e.g. by accepting ancient myths at face value).

In these ways, the self-defined Celts can be said to form an
ethnic group.

It is a rather extraordinary argument. Half of these 'Celts',
in Scotland and Wales, have often been happy to define themselves as 'British', meaning a member of the political-cultural
amalgam of Great Britain. In Ireland, two 'Celtic' communities have been at loggerheads over religion, a central attribute
of culture. There is more than a hint of mental and spiritual
laziness among the many who parade a Celtic identity, compared with the few who actually speak and use the remaining
Celtic languages. James rather gives up his effort at justifica-
tion by admitting that:

'. . . perhaps the clearest evidence for the reality of the *modern* insular Celts is the simple fact that millions of people
feel themselves to be in some way Celtic.'

Proud as it is, that label can only be misleading. It does no justice
to the immensely long continuity of life in the islands. Before
ever the Greeks adopted the term *keltoi* for a continental group of
peoples, the inhabitants of prehistoric Ireland and Britain were
evolving a distinctive way of life, establishing their own places
and markers in the landscape, giving it names, making it yield
sustenance and raw material for their benefit. Whatever the later

additions and admixtures to that population – and there were many, from the displaced Belgae of Flanders to the Roman legionary veterans from Dacia and Sarmatia, who settled on their pension-farms; to the Angles, Jutes, and Saxons, and the motley collection of larger or smaller immigrant groups who came after them: Danes, Norwegians, Normans, Bretons, Flemings, Jews, Huguenot French, Palatinate Germans, Jamaicans, Nigerians, Ugandan-Asians, Bengalis, and more – these forefathers and foremothers, a hybrid lot themselves, form a long tradition of human occupancy. The culture of the islands' peoples has gone through many phases, always subject to strong influence from outside, always preserving older and local elements.

Unfortunately, 'island peoples' is not a very satisfying or reso-nant title to apply to such a vibrant section of humanity. 'British' has acquired an altered and restrictive meaning. 'Celtic' has shown great resilience and, however much the pedantic histo-rian may carp, it is not going to go away. Rather the opposite. In a curious way, however, it has outgrown the islands that claimed it. One of the most remarkable things about this term is how it has acquired an additional range of latter-day connotations to do with ecological awareness, sensitivity to the natural world, spiri-tual penetration and general otherworldliness. W. B. Yeats and 'Fiona McLeod' and other proponents of the 'Celtic twilight' are the godfathers of this development and would no doubt be pleased by it. George Buchanan and Edward Lhuyd would be horrified, one suspects. But, approve of it or not, the modern 'Celtic' spirit goes marching serenely on its way, waving its dif-ferent flags, decked with streamers of tartan and saffron, embla-zoned with thistles, shamrocks and leeks, and proclaiming its sometimes contradictory identities to the accompanying strains of bagpipe, tin whistle, and harp. In the surrounding mists, the attendant figures of shamanists, tantric yogists, cosmic-power tappers, grail theorists, seekers of the inner self, and the advo-cates of a dozen kinds of meditation, massage, or mystic com-munion come and go. One can only wish it well.

Tribal Groups in the British Isles, 70–300CE

The map on page 186 shows the approximate locations of known tribal groups inhabiting the British Isles during the period from 70CE to 300CE. The information comes from chiefly from Ptolemy's *Geography* and Latin sources. A few words of caution are necessary. It will be immediately obvious that several tribes are shown as located in a region of which very little is known: Scotland north and west of the Great Glen. These names are from Ptolemy and little or nothing is known for sure about their background. They do not appear in later Pictish or Scottish regional names. Still in Scotland, it has been noted in the main text how names have varied from century to century, with the Maeatae and Verturiones found where Tacitus, in the first century, mentions only Caledonii. Among the tribes of England, ancient historians have thought that the number of small groups noted in the northern area, like the Carvetii and the Textoverdi, may be subdivisions of the much larger group of the Brigantes, emerging into independence under a strong ruler. This assumes the Brigantes to have been more of a federation than a single tribe. There were Irish Brigantes also, and the Gangani are found both in Ireland and in Wales. The Darini of northeast Ireland have been linked by some scholars with the Dàl Araidhe tribal group, related to the Cruithin or Picts.

Ptolemy was a methodical and reliable geographer and it can

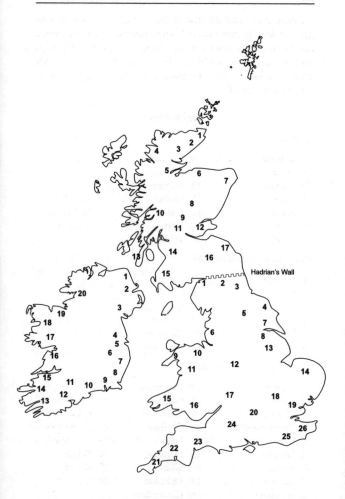

reasonably be assumed that all his names are based on evidence judged by him to have been satisfactory, meaning from a first-hand source, even if it was already an old one. The gaps on the map, most notable in the islands, do not necessarily imply that there were no inhabitants, but simply that no information was available.

Key to Map

Hibernia

1. Robogdi or Redodii	8. Coriondi	15. Luceni
2. Darini	9. Menapii	16. Gangani
3. Voluntii	10. Brigantes	17. Auteini
4. Ebdani	11. Vodiae	18. Nagnate
5. Blanii	12. Uterni	19. Dumnonii
6. Usdiae	13. Iverni	20. Vennicni
7. Cauci	14. Velabri	

Britain, north of Hadrian's Wall

1. Cornavii	7. Taezali	13. Epidii
2. Lugi	8. Caledonii	14. Damnonii
3. Smertae	9. Carnonaceae	15. Novantae
4. Caereni	10. Creones	16. Selgovae
5. Decantae	11. Vacomagi	17. Votadini
6. Boresti	12. Venicones	

Britain, south of Hadrian's Wall

1. Caretii	10. Deceangli	19. Trinovantes
2. Lopocares	11. Ordovices	20. Atrebates
3. Textoverdi	12. Cornovii	21. Cornavii
4. Gabrantovices	13. Coritani	22. Dumnonii
5. Brigantes	14. Iceni	23. Durotriges
6. Setantii	15. Demetae	24. Belgae
7. Parisii	16. Silures	25. Regini
8. Cassi	17. Dobunni	26. Cantiaci
9. Gangani	18. Catuvellauni	

APPENDIX 2

Select Bibliography

Black, R., Gillies, W., and Ò Maolalaigh, R., *Celtic Connections*. Phantassie, 1999

Chadwick, Nora, *The Celts* (new ed.). London, 1997

Chapman, Malcolm, *The Celts*. London, 1992

Cunliffe, Barry, *The Ancient Celts*. London, 1999

Dillon, Myles, and Chadwick, Nora, *The Celtic Realms*. London, 1967

Durkacz, Victor Edward, *The Decline of the Celtic Languages*. Edinburgh, 1983

Dyer, James, *Ancient Britain*. London, 1990

Foster, Sally, *Picts, Gaels and Scots*. London, 1996

Hubert, Henri, *The Rise of the Celts* (revised 1934). London, 1987

James, Simon, *The Atlantic Celts*. London, 1999

Koch, J.T., and Carey, J., *The Celtic Heroic Age*. Malden, Mass., 1995

Kruta, Venceslas, *The Celts of the West*. London, 1985

MacKillop, James, *Dictionary of Celtic Mythology*. Oxford, 1998

Malone, Caroline, *Neolithic Britain and Ireland*. Stroud, 2001

O'Kelly, Michael, *Early Ireland*. Cambridge, 1989

Renfrew, Colin, *Archaeology and Language*. London, 1987

Ross, Anne, *Pagan Celtic Britain*. London, 1971

Salway, Peter, *Roman Britain*. Oxford, 1981